What people are saying about L. Carol Scott

Carol is one of the most authentic people I know. Her honesty, humanity, and willingness to share the deepest parts of herself facilitate understanding and healing for others. For decades, she has been a fierce advocate and teacher for children (including my own). Her life is a testament of healing and empowerment for others.

—Majida Watkins Foster, parent

This book is like a gift you give to yourself on behalf of those who love you. It's a guide on how to look in a mirror and better understand, appreciate, and love the person looking back at you. It's a bit like a make-your-own-adventure book, where the real adventure is yourself.

—Dr. Walter Gilliam, Director
Edward Zigler Center in Child Development
and Social Policy, Yale University

After Carol's workshop series, I saw that I had only begun to unearth the gems beneath the surface. With each Treasure mined, I became more aware of myself, and the many ways I had yet to unfold. We were guided with such grace and ease into opening these doors for ourselves. Carol's approach is soft, warm, authentic, and comfortable. Knowing that she, too, has been doing and continues to do the work, I felt understood at a level that allowed me to be vulnerable enough to grow. I now claim a stronger, more confident, less encumbered Me.

—Rev. Jacquie Burge
Workshop participant

just be YOUR S.E.L.F.*

YOUR GUIDE TO IMPROVING ANY RELATIONSHIP

L. Carol Scott, PhD

✶ Self-governed•Ego-aware•Leading•Free

Big Dream Press

Just Be Your S.E.L.F.
Your Guide to Improving Any Relationship
Dr. L. Carol Scott, PhD
Big Dream Press

Published by Big Dream Press, St. Louis, MO
Copyright ©2018 Dr. L.Carol Scott, PhD
All rights reserved.

No part of this publication may be reproduced, stored in a retrieval system, or transmitted in any form or by any means, electronic, mechanical, photocopying, recording, scanning, or otherwise, except as permitted under Section 107 or 108 of the 1976 United States Copyright Act, without the prior written permission of the Publisher. Requests to the Publisher for permission should be addressed to Permissions Department, Big Dream Press at carol @lcarolscott.com

Limit of Liability/Disclaimer of Warranty: While the publisher and author have used their best efforts in preparing this book, they make no representations or warranties with respect to the accuracy or completeness of the contents of this book and specifically disclaim any implied warranties of merchantability or fitness for a particular purpose. No warranty may be created or extended by sales representatives or written sales materials. The advice and strategies contained herein may not be suitable for your situation. You should consult with a professional where appropriate. Neither the publisher nor author shall be liable for any loss of profit or any other commercial damages, including but not limited to special, incidental, consequential, or other damages.

Names, characters, businesses, places, events and incidents are either the products of the author's imagination or used in a fictitious manner. Any resemblance to actual persons, living or dead, or actual events is purely coincidental.

Editor: Karen Tucker, CommaQueenEditing.com

Cover and Interior design: Davis Creative, DavisCreative.com

Library of Congress Cataloging-in-Publication Data

Library of Congress Control Number: 2018910411

Author Dr. L. Carol Scott, PhD

Just Be Your S.E.L.F.: Your Guide to Improving Any Relationship

ISBN: 978-1-7326452-0-2

Library of Congress subject headings:

    1. SEL016000 SELF-HELP / Personal Growth / Happiness   2. SEL027000 SELF-HELP / Personal Growth / Success   3. SEL044000 SELF-HELP / Self-Management / General

2018

ATTENTION CORPORATIONS, UNIVERSITIES, COLLEGES AND PROFESSIONAL ORGANIZATIONS: Quantity discounts are available on bulk purchases of this book for educational, gift purposes, or as premiums for increasing magazine subscriptions or renewals. Special books or book excerpts can also be created to fit specific needs. For information, please contact Big Dream Press, PO Box 1122, Maryland Heights, MO 63043; ph 866.665.5569.

*For the children
of America*

Acknowledgments

This book is, in significant ways, a reflection of my life to date. So, I begin my thanks with my father, who may be a controversial choice for some readers. Yet I cannot deny that I am who I am today largely because he stole my innocence, my sense of physical safety, and—for so many years—a wholeness of personality, a self. Those are the lemons from which I made this lemonade that is my life. Along with him, I thank my whole extended family for the parts they played in the dramas and traumas of my childhood and my subsequent recovery. Even when they hurt more than helped, they gave me opportunities to grow. As a standout among the helpers, I want to honor my Uncle Kenneth Scott. When I "came out" to my family as a victim of father incest, Uncle Ken believed me without question and supported me, unconditionally and wholeheartedly, despite his longstanding close relationship with my father. I will always be grateful for that validation in what felt like a riptide of doubt, distance, and judgment from so many.

Profound thanks go to my mother, as my first and last writing teacher, and to all the writing teachers in between, especially Ms. Donnis Boyce at Shawnee Mission South and Dr. Don Bushell Jr. at the University of Kansas. I thank my grandfather, Al Kastman, for financing the first four years of my higher education and other financial support that enriched my childhood and young adulthood in many ways.

For the guidance that led me into the study of and a profession in child development, I thank Divine Love. It always knows and wants the best for me.

With heartfelt gratitude, I acknowledge Dr. Marilyn Hutchinson, the gifted therapist who led me down the early miles of my journey to wholeness. With her, I also honor the women of her weekly incest survivors' therapy groups (one of which she co-facilitated with Dr. Susan Brandt) and the women in the peer group for addiction recovery I co-facilitated at Lavender Umbrella in the late 1980s. Marilyn's and Susan's skills, knowledge, and compassion, and the love and courage of all those fellow survivors and addicts—all focused on their healing and wholeness—were significant medicine for mine.

I am thankful to Cynthia Jones, cofounder of Diana's Grove, all the members of its Mystery Schools from 1999 through 2007, and others who attended Grove events in 2004–2007, at which I offered my earliest workshops on what became the *7 Childhood Treasures* model. My integration of learning from Cynthia's writings and the responses of my Grove workshop participants shaped my early understanding of how to share knowledge of developmental milestones through tools of personal transformation.

Over the 10 years between that early development of the Treasures and now, I have continued to do my recovery and healing work, toward greater and greater wholeness of personality, using the ***7 Childhood Treasures*** tools I offer in this book. I've continued to offer workshops, refining my tools and honing my message. I am particularly grateful for the generous response from the loving community at the Center for Spiritual Living–St. Louis during these recent years and to many professional colleagues who encouraged my efforts. Everyone who committed to the 7 Treasures work and found it healing contributed to my understanding of my own healing and to my ability to bring this healing work to wider audiences.

The tribe of family, friends, and followers that patiently supported me through all these decades of trauma and recovery have now concretely supported my dream to bring this book to the world with their investments in a Kickstarter campaign. For this very powerful manifestation miracle, I thank and honor these 90 longtime friends, new friends, family members, coworkers, colleagues, and loved ones:

Extraordinary Investments
- Heidi Bayer
- Janikka Rene Garrity
- Craig Scott
- Steve Smith
- Wendi Whiles

Vision Level
- Jessica Adams
- Sue Baxter
- Kathy Fridge
- John Greenleaf
- Macha Greenleaf
- Jack & Gerry Kastman
- Amy Markley-Watson
- Joy Weese Moll
- Ken Percy
- Steve, Christine, & Ava Sohnrey
- Patrice TenBroek
- Richard & Nancy Tichenor
- Marcia Walton

Faith Level
- Jeanne Adwani
- Holly Anderson
- Mark Baxter
- Chris Carosella
- Jason Collins
- Julee Higginbotham
- Jo Howard
- Sue Kuda
- Linda Moen
- Rebecca Nottingham
- Steve O'Rourke
- Paulita Pranschke
- Mickey Robertaccio
- Cori Scheitlin
- Diane Schurr
- Janika Scott
- Lincoln Scott
- Mike Seiwert
- Jodi Sonderman

Trust Level

Carla Adams
Anna Allen
Barbara Altman
Christian Baxter
Maria Bon Durant
Stephane Brewster
Lisa Bruce
Amy Cranch
Jane Cothron
Kathryn "Kitty" Degler
Cindy Dehner
Amber Donnelly
Christopher Dork
Lilian Due
Donna Farber
Constance Fleming
Majida Foster
Debbie Frazin
Liz Graham*
Melissa Heston
Brenda Boda Klenke
Judy Lemon
Suzi McFarland
Bo McGuire
Rebecca Now
Epiphany Paris
Barb Pitcher
Jen Price
Brenda Reed
Renee Richards
Laurie Staples Ritchie
Katherine Roccasecca
Pat Ruble
Amy Scheiderman
Marti Sittner
Bridget Smith
Solice & Adam
Teri Parsley Starnes
Alyson Taggart
Annette Thornton
Elizabeth Townsend
Diane Van Dyke
Cindy Van Hooser
Monice Van Steenberg
Marilyn Sue Warren
Bobbi Wells
Pamela Wilz
BeBe Wood

*A note of special honor to Liz, who made the first pledge in the Kickstarter campaign.

Because no author births a book alone, I share my deep gratitude to my fabulous partners, Jack and Cathy Davis of Davis Creative, for "getting" my mission, inspiration and design for developing my brand, publication design and layout, support for the publication process, and boosting my signal. I also thank Julie Hohe of Hohe Virtual Assistant Services for communications support, Karen Tucker of Comma Queen Editing, and Victor de Castro of User King for excellent web support.

Last but certainly not least, I thank you, dear reader, for taking this book into your hands and giving it your attention. You have just become another partner in my mission to change the way we treat children in America. Bless you for that!

Contents

Preface xi
Why This Book? 1
Life Without Your *7 Childhood Treasures* 5
Who We Are Meant to Be 7
Your Little Red House 9
The Challenge of Being Your S.E.L.F. 11
Choosing Your S.E.L.F. 13
A S.E.L.F. Enters the World 15
    Result Number One: Your Life is Your Choice 16
    Result Number Two: You Know You Have Agency 16
    Result Number Three: You Take Responsibility 17
The *7 Childhood Treasures* and How They Grow 19
    What is Trust? 23
    What is Independence? 25
    What is Faith? 28
    What is Negotiation? 30
    What is Vision? 33
    What is Compromise? 35
    What is Acceptance? 37
Struggling Without the *7 Childhood Treasures*? 41
Got Treasures? 45
Good News! It's Never Too Late to Mine! 51
A Final Reminder 53
Find Your Trust 55
    Trust Who for What? 57
Excavate Your Independence 65
    Moon Boundaries 67
    Question Reality 70
Gather Your Faith 75
    Someone Could 77
    Be the White Queen 80

Mine Your Negotiation **85**
    Negotiation Boxes 88
    What do you want? 93
Cut the Facets of Your Vision **97**
    Map of Promise..99
Smooth Out Your Compromise **105**
    The Power of Choice 107
    Guided Choice 108
    Value-Driven Compromise.........................112
Polish Up Your Acceptance **115**
    Surrender Betrayal 118
    An Altar to Betrayal 122
    Values Revisited 123
Life With Your 7 Childhood Treasures **125**
    A Day in the Life of a S.E.L.F. 125
Just Be Your S.E.L.F. **129**
About the Author **131**

Preface

I'm so glad you're here, starting this book. You know why? Because I want for you the same kind of joy, freedom, and creativity I've found. I want you to feel excited about your life every day because the pure potential of you is embraced in all your important relationships.

Welcome to the world of the *7 Childhood Treasures*. I created this framework to draw seven brightly colored connections between your early development and your current success in relationships. While your first seven years may seem like an odd source of guidance for getting along in your twenties and beyond, you can trust me that it's really the only source of guidance that makes any sense at all.

As a developmental psychologist and national leader in early care and education, I hold no other truth to be as self-evident as this one: The first seven years of your life were deterministic in their creation of who you are now. Far beyond a "shaping" factor or "influence," those early years define you. Your fundamental social and emotional infrastructure, out of which you create all your future relationships, is literally hard-wired into your brain from birth to age seven.

Which takes us to the question, why me? What do I have to offer you that no other early education expert can? Well, I used my understanding of early development to re-create my outcomes from those years. I literally rewired my brain. Understanding how a child learns to trust in the first few months of life, and how a toddler finds her boundaries of "self," allowed me to mimic those processes and find healthier trust and boundaries myself. For every one of the *7 Childhood Treasures*, I followed this process.

Of this I am deeply certain: If I can do it, so can you. I grew up in a family affected by many of what we now call Adverse Childhood Experiences: parental alcoholism, sexual abuse, verbal and emotional abuse, divorce, and financial strain. Blessed also with many resilience factors—neighbors, teachers, and others who provided balance for the stressors—and my own indomitable spirit, I survived it all, as well as the self-destructive, acting-out behavior of my young adulthood.

Having forgiven myself for every crazy way I acted out my pain, I have no judgment for any of yours. Bring yourself, as you are, to this work, and trust the process of your own healing and becoming. The effort is worth it, more than you can even imagine right now.

See you in the mine shafts, tools in hand,

L Carol Scott

Why This Book?

The title says it all and I'm not kidding. I just want you to be yourself. This book serves what I hope is already your purpose: to be the best possible version of *you*. Why this book? To help you fully express your potential: the innate and unique value only you can bring to the world. As the beloved Dr. Seuss said in his book, *Happy Birthday to You*, "There is no one alive who is you-er than you."

This book is for you if you're living any life in which you feel less than brimming with unbridled joy and energetic effectiveness most of the time. That joyless life, that flat life, that weary, angry, lost, or sad life—those are NOT the lives you were created to lead. You were not conceived—whether you believe it was by Divinity or science—to be desperate, sad, bored, angry, ineffective, and unsuccessful throughout your life…AND you don't have to be. The good news is that it's never too late to stop walking the path you've been on and start a new path. This book aims to lead you through a set of massive "do-overs." You can start, right now, creating the freedom to fully express the gift to the world that is you.

The work I offer in my ***7 Childhood Treasures*** workshops and classes is a lovely means to that end. If you want to give and receive all the possible good in your own life, and empower others to do the same, you want these shining gems in your life: Trust, Independence, Faith, Negotiation, Vision, Compromise, and Acceptance.

What am I talking about? Volumes of theory and research evidence agree, as do the folk wisdom traditions in many cultures, that the first seven years create a child's foundation. Consolidating the theory and research, I have identified seven essential assets for a successful adult life full of purpose and joy, all meant to be acquired within the first seven years of life. Each of us enters the world preprogrammed to develop these assets and a life that is free, self-governed, and accountable. Each of us is capable of growing into an adult who has healthy, loving, supportive relationships full of mutual respect and generosity of spirit, at home, at work, and in the wider public arenas in which we live our lives.

So, why do so many of us settle for lives of quiet frustration? Why do we put up with loved ones who don't seem to see or hear us? who hurt us? Why do we put on a happy face for the public while we grieve over a giant black hole of loss, the origin of which we do not understand?

You may never have experienced a relationship that meets your needs, respects your boundaries, engages you in dreams of the future, and allows you to negotiate for what you want. If that is the case, how can you grieve the loss of *that* kind of relationship?

I'll say it again: Each of us is capable of becoming an adult who has healthy, loving, supportive relationships full of mutual respect and generosity of spirit. Unfortunately, most of us came through those first seven years without the support needed to fully realize all that potential.

Possibly, even probably, we didn't have "bad" parents. I mean, lots of you had parents who never hit you or said demeaning or insulting things to you, never sexually assaulted you, never shamed you in public, were never even a little bit cruel to you. Lots and lots of people had pretty good parents who were still truly clueless about how to foster development of those essential assets for healthy adult relationships.

Yes, you can have pretty good parents and still have messy, fraught, and downright torturous relationships as an adult. Yes, you can be pretty messed up as an adult, even after a decent childhood.

And then there are the millions of us whose early years were pummeled by brutal forces: poverty, hunger, neglect, trauma, cruelty witnessed, or violence endured. These Adverse Childhood Experiences (ACEs), as they've come to be known, have long-term and serious effects on adult well-being, including both mental and physical health. Even without trauma like violence, the daily toxic stress in many households experiencing poverty or adult substance abuse is considered an ACE.

Any of these kinds of early childhood experiences could have limited or completely stymied your ability to mine those precious ores of possibility within you. Many kinds of childhoods could have led you straight into a bevy of adult relationships riddled with unnecessary drama or negativity, dissatisfied desires for emotional intimacy and respect, or even abuse in one or more of its various forms.

You could be living a life of quiet desperation, or one of top-volume regret, feeling your choices are limited and your future dim or grim. You could be filled with sadness, feeling that you have no ability to get what you want in life or to make the impact you dreamed of long ago.

If you are among those who live with this drama, dissatisfaction, grim regret, or sadness, then you're the answer to "Why this book?"

You can reclaim your birthright of the ***7 Childhood Treasures***, those seven assets that were preprogrammed into you. Those raw ores are still there, buried now under a slag heap of life experiences. Your family couldn't hand you the tools to mine them, shape their many facets, and polish their luster. And you still can drill down and find them. Start now. It's never too late.

The mining effort needed to relocate those ores and transform them into the jewels you need *may* take every bit of seven years. For those of us whose childhood ACEs were deeply damaging, the work of recovering your **7 Childhood Treasures** may become a longer occupation, and I can testify that the time investment is worth it! Even making a start will change your life for the better, right here and right now.

If you want to be your S.E.L.F., you can.

Being your S.E.L.F. awakens passion in your life, unlocks potential within yourself, opens the door to your abundance, and delivers joy—the highest form of love. Indeed, focusing on leading our own lives could change the *whole* world if enough of us made this commitment.

Here's the truth as I see it: You can feel free to choose your direction, confident of your ability to achieve your dreams and full to overflowing with love and generosity. You can leave behind any regrets or sense of defeat as you claim your life in this new way.

Sound good? Let's go!

Life Without Your 7 Childhood Treasures

First, what do relationship interactions look like when neither of the participants has mined these Treasures? Here are a few snapshots:

Starting the Day. Partner A, seemingly out-of-the-blue and in a bit of a strangled voice, hollers from the bathroom, "Did you return-ship that shirt yesterday like I asked you to?" Partner B, reacting to the bizarre tone of voice, angrily hollers back from the bedroom next door, "Why do you never trust me to do what I say I will?" Partner A yells even louder, "Oh, please. Like you trust me? And why do you have to make *every* little thing into a fight ALL the time?"

Settling in at Work. Employee, flying a bit breathlessly into a chair at exactly the start time of the sales meeting, sees Manager frowning. Frowning back, Employee says, "You did SAY it was okay to be late today. Did you forget?" Manager glowers, checking his calendar, before giving a curt reply of, "Right. Next time remind me the day before." For the rest of the meeting, Employee's comments are either ignored by Manager or dismissed as irrelevant.

Morning Break. Coworker A slides into a group around a table and whispers, "Did you hear about J____ from Marketing stealing office supplies?" Coworker B replies in a conspiratorial whisper, "OMG! No! Tell me everything!!" Within minutes, they have gathered a cluster of coworkers who are gossiping about several other employees, including J___ from Marketing. J___ then walks in and overhears them.

Morning Team Meeting. Team Leader opens the agenda with a need to course-correct on a goal that is not on target to be achieved. Team Leader asks for suggested new strategies to reach the goal, and Team Member offers a three-step plan that seems to address the barriers in the current plan. In the conversation that follows, the team significantly modifies the middle of the three steps, and a group consensus builds around the revised version of the plan. Team Leader affirms the new plan and asks Team Member, "Do you have any comments on the modifications to your suggested plan?" Team Member responds, in a voice shaking with emotion, "I don't understand why you guys never like my ideas."

Lunch. Friends meet for a planning session for their upcoming cruise to Alaska. Each brings a vision of ideas, the special sites, or events of interest of highest priority, and each has a lot of investment in that vision. After an hour of mostly dancing around their differences and arguing, they leave without a clear plan, wondering why they're going on a cruise together when they're so different.

Afternoon Appointment. Colleague A and Colleague B meet to design a new workflow. Colleague A is testy and defensive, signaling his ideas are the best and need no discussion. Colleague B, wishing to avoid conflict and drama, but filled with resentment, agrees to everything A proposes.

Evening Workout. After work at the gym, Body Builder approaches the only ab crunch machine at the same time as Wellness Seeker. Builder asks Seeker if he'd be willing to let him go first because he needs to pick up his children from child care by 6:30 or pay for overtime. Seeker curtly replies, "I was here first," and takes a seat on the machine.

Family Dinner. Adult Child comes over for dinner with Parent, who has worked hard for hours to prepare a delicious meal of favorite childhood dishes the Child no longer eats, having chosen a vegan diet. Child spends the meal picking at the food, criticizing the dietary habits of Parent.

TV Time. Friends have a plan to watch a movie together at Host's home. Ignoring the past chronic pattern of Visitor arriving late, Host prepares some fancy, labor-intensive snacks that must be eaten as soon as they come out of the oven. Visitor, predictably, is late. The snacks are ruined. Host texts Visitor, "Don't bother to come now, you jerk. I'm watching the movie without you."

Going to Bed. As they both settle in for the night, going through their bedtime routines, Partner A asks Partner B, "What's your day like tomorrow?" Partner B growls back, "What do you want me to do for you now, and why can't you run your own errands, dammit?"

Now we turn out the light on a day missing the protection of all *7 Childhood Treasures*. Tomorrow, we begin to create a different approach to life, being a **S**elf-governed, **E**go-aware, **L**eading, Free **S.E.L.F.**

Who We Are Meant to Be

I'm a developmental psychologist, so my professional point of view encompasses the genetic and environmental factors that influence human development. My role is to explain how those factors shape us and make us who we are. How we grow and become who we *are* is my area of study and work and also my passion. For decades of my career, the question of who we were **meant to become** didn't even come into my field of intellectual vision. And then, one day, it did. From that day to this one, there has been no more important question for me to explore.

For a time, I ran beside the question, "Who are we meant to be?" striving to keep up with all the paths it traveled. Finally, I found what I believe to be an answer: I am meant, you are meant, all of us are meant to be *fully* ourselves. We are meant to be in charge of our lives. Not the whole of life, or even the whole of one's world. My choices are mine, for my life, and are not expected of the friends, family members, other loved ones, neighbors, and coworkers who populate my world. I expect them each to be themselves and lead their lives as well.

Why is "Your S.E.L.F." my answer to the question, "Who are you meant to be?" Simple: because each of us is programmed for that end. Each of us is born with the raw ores of seven assets specifically designed to help us express a unique S.E.L.F. Coincidentally, they also program us for the skills and dispositions to get along with other unique selves.

How about that?

The literature of developmental psychology—both theory and research—clearly reveals that we are intended to gather these assets that lead to a self-governed, aware life. Whatever your belief system—whether it is that evolution wants us to be a whole S.E.L.F. or a higher being does—the truth is that the raw ores were there, within you, when you were born. If unmined and unrefined in your early years, then they are still there, waiting for you.

These **7 Childhood Treasures** are buried in our genetic programming, ready to be brought into the personality structure we build from birth, each on a scheduled timeline. Whether those potential gems were fully mined, cut, and polished to enable a S.E.L.F. depends entirely on the caregiving, parenting, and education in our early lives. Parents, grandparents, siblings, teachers, and other influential adults and older youth in our lives had the task of helping us mine for these Treasures. They gave us the tools and supported our work in building a home for S.E.L.F.—or they didn't. More on that in a minute.

So now you know that you came into this life with raw materials to develop the *7 Childhood Treasures*, the fine arts of:

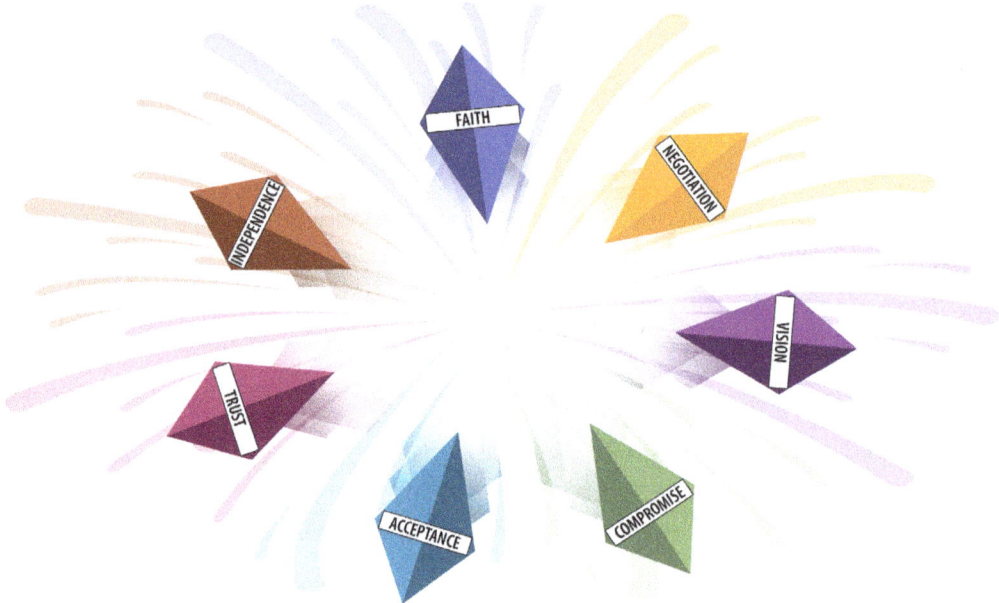

Now that you know that, what's next?

Your Little Red House

I invite you into a story—an aide to your understanding and memory—because the human mind *loves* stories! In this story, your **7 Childhood Treasures** are magically strong components of an important building: the home for your S.E.L.F. They anchor the foundation and key joints in the structure, bringing stability and the kind of flexible strength that withstands the earthquakes, hurricanes, and tornadoes of adult relationships.

Imagine a small house, as drawn by a child. A square holds the living space, and a triangle on top is the roof. Seven connection points—four in the square and three more in the roof—secure the shelter.

Using this Little Red House as our metaphor, imagine with me that the Treasure of Trust is one of the cornerstones at the bottom of the square. It anchors the left bottom corner of the square, while Independence anchors it on the right. These first two gems act as pedestals holding up each side of the home of your S.E.L.F. They are as essential to holding you up in life as a concrete foundation is to holding up a house.

Directly above Trust is the Treasure of Faith at the left upper corner of the square. Faith secures the top point for the left wall of your Little Red House. On the right side of the square, directly above Independence, Negotiation holds up that wall. These positions are not random! Faith relies on Trust as its foundation, and the capacity for Negotiation rests on the mental, emotional, and other boundaries of Independence.

Those first four Treasures hold the corners of the square living space in your Little Red House. The bottom edge of your home's little triangular roof is anchored by two more Treasures: Vision on the left and Compromise on the right. These new additions create the ability to cap off your personality's home. Your capacity for Vision rests on a sturdy underpinning of Trust and Faith. Compromise needs beneath it the support of your Independence and your capacity for Negotiation.

Finally, the top of the triangle—the roof peak of your Little Red House—is the Treasure of Acceptance. Literally impossible without the other six Treasures beneath for structural support, the tiny triangular tip of the roof represents this capacity. Ironically, that tiny sparkling anchor point at the top of the roof is what keeps out most of life's bad weather.

With these Treasures in the foundation and infrastructure of your personality's home, you become your **S.E.L.F.**—**S**elf-governed, **E**go-aware, **L**eading your life, and **F**ree.

The End.

There it is: the little story of a home for your personality. I invite you to lightly carry this mental model through the rest of this book-long journey. A mental model is simply a graphic image that helps you remember a set of complex but related points. The key points to remember with the Little Red House are:

- Trust and Independence are your foundation.
- Faith relies on Trust to support it.
- Negotiation cannot be successful without Independence.
- Vision balances on top of Trust and Faith.
- Compromise balances on top of Independence and Negotiation.
- Acceptance is impossible without the other six and protects them all.

The Challenge of Being Your S.E.L.F.

Although you entered life with a full supply of raw rock from which to mine the **Childhood Treasures**, it's a big, multiyear job. In fact, it's designed to take seven years. You needed tools and some help to mine, cut, and polish these jewels. Those tools and that help could have, *should* have, come from the adults who parented and educated you.

Your genetic readiness to be yourself can only be actualized by others' interactions with you as you grow up. If early interactions consistently or often ignored or minimized your value; if you were belittled, controlled, demeaned, or dismissed; or if people who were supposed to help you actually hurt you, then your Treasures are still buried and waiting for you.

For now, you may need to just believe me when I tell you that, no matter how good your parents were to you, they likely *did* devalue you, probably many times. They may not have *meant* to devalue you, but they did. Most of us who grew up in American households did so with our "self" unacknowledged, our unique value denied or minimized, often and from a very tender age. Your parents likely didn't mean to hurt you; it's just what mainstream American parenting has been like, back many generations to its European roots.

Growing up this way doesn't necessarily mean we had bad parents, evil parents, or parents to blame for all the ills of our lives. What we had were *human* parents, reared in a particular culture. They, too, did not become a S.E.L.F. We had parents who grew up with *their* value unwittingly denied or minimized by their parents (i.e., your grandparents), who also missed becoming a S.E.L.F. On and on it goes, back into our histories, generations of not knowing the truth of who we are meant to be.

I know it's hard to hear, but it's certainly true. We can only change it if we are willing to face the reality head on. Unwittingly devaluing our children is a cultural norm in the U.S. and has been for many generations.

This book will offer you many specific examples of this cultural norm of casually and chronically devaluing young children. To get us started, here are just a few, fairly benign examples:
- Passing a newborn around a group of adults who babble, gurgle, cuddle, and coo over her without noticing her repeated and escalating signals that she is overstimulated and needs a rest.
- Letting a six-month-old cry himself to sleep so he won't become "spoiled."
- Requiring a toddler to share her toys so she'll learn manners.
- Laughing at a young preschooler's "silly" belief in fairies.
- Refusing a four-year-old's efforts to reasonably negotiate what he eats for lunch.
- Telling a preschooler that it's not possible for her to use her blocks to build a tower taller than her house.
- Refusing a kindergartner's request with the rationale, "Because I said so."
- Asserting that a fellow second grader who hurt your child's feelings is "just a bad person."

Choosing Your S.E.L.F.

We live as ourselves when we are consciously in charge of how we show up in the world, when we *choose* our lives. You may believe you already choose your behavior. Do you also believe, at least sometimes, that others are to blame for how you act? Have you ever heard yourself say someone else made you do something you didn't want to or wouldn't let you do something you did want to do?

Even if you're clear and conscious about choosing your actions, do you know you also choose your thoughts and feelings? Truly, nobody else can make the choices that create your life. As the leaders in our lives, we are *meant* to make them.

The rest of us around you—your parents/grandparents/siblings, teachers/mentors, friends, partners, and coworkers—we can support you. We can be courageous enough to honestly tell you how your choices affect us, both the positive impacts and those that hurt us or attempt to limit our choices. We can encourage you to reflect on your experiences and learn from them. We can even help you learn by asking thoughtful, real questions or by sharing our own experiences of reflective learning. We can be good role models for living as our unique selves. We can comfort you when your choices have consequences that hurt you.

But YOU, and only you, make the choices that govern your life. When it *appears* that others make your choices for you, you wind up living a pseudo-life: neither yours nor theirs. And the truth is that when others seem to be making your choices, you *are* choosing…to do or feel what someone else thinks you should do or feel. Maybe your choice is made to make someone else happy. Maybe you "choose" to avoid making someone else unhappy or angry. Regardless, none of these "choices" is a promising route to being your S.E.L.F.

Personal sovereignty, which is ego-aware self-governance, is how you're meant to live. You are meant to consciously choose how to think, feel, and act. You are meant to hear about your impact on others and to use that feedback for learning about how to be your best self. From your earliest years of life, you are meant to learn the dual arts of making, and living with, your choices.

You are meant to start small when you are a toddler, practicing toddler choices like what to eat, what to wear, or where to sit. As a preschooler, you are meant to expand your skills and understanding, making choices about how to express your needs and desires, what strategies to use to get what you want, or how to navigate in a small group of friends.

Are you surprised to hear that you're genetically programmed for all of this? There's more.

The older you get, the more complex your choices become. If you were denied age-appropriate self-governance as a toddler and preschooler, you likely were ill-prepared for this increasing complexity. If someone else chose your clothes, food, activities, and friends when you were young, how well-prepared could you have been to choose your morals, manners, career, and life partner?

Yet these choices must be made, either by you or "for" you. I fervently hope that the family or families in which you grew up helped you find your birthright: a generative and rewarding life full of purpose and joy, relationships with family and friends that are rich with emotional intimacy and mutual honoring of one another's sovereignty, and an abiding peace with your contributions to life.

You have only to look around you, or read or listen to what passes for news today, to see that the world is not full of such relationships. Sadly, most of us grew up in flawed, wounded, doing-the-best-they-could-with-the-tools-they-had families, repeating mistakes handed down generation by generation without even knowing they were mistakes.

Here's what I need you to know right now: Those mistakes don't need to have permanent results.

I'm going to say that again in another way. The echoes from your childhood are not meant to become the soundtrack for your adult life. It's time for a do-over of your early years.

If you, like me, grew up with little or no awareness of S.E.L.F., there is hope now. If you, like me, suffered trauma from abuse and/or grew up with drug- or alcohol-addicted parents, who had no hope of honoring any child's uniqueness, there is still hope for you now. If you were reared by adults who suffered from depression, bipolar disorder, obsessive-compulsive disorder, or a host of other psychological woes, you can still have a S.E.L.F. now.

All you must do is decide to start. Now! You can choose self-governance right now and build a Treasure-anchored Little Red House from which to lead a free life, starting right now.

Maybe you've known for a while that you need to be more "in charge" of your life, or maybe you're still denying there's a problem. Whenever and however you become aware that self-governance is a missing essential in your life (Hey, maybe that's right now!), you will find you have some growing to do. You will need to develop the art of choice-making that you didn't develop in those early years. You will need to work to accumulate the assets that enable this personal sovereignty.

That's where this book comes in!

You could have/should have mined the ***7 Childhood Treasures***, these assets to build the Little Red House that safely contains and protects your S.E.L.F., in the first seven years of your life. If you didn't, it is never too late to start. This book serves as a guide for that process.

A S.E.L.F. Enters the World

In my framework of the Treasures, five-year-old children develop the Treasure of Vision, which includes the lesson that before we begin any journey, it's important to have a destination in mind. If I just start walking, I will surely end up somewhere, but is it where I wanted to be?

Let's take a look at the destination for this book's journey. How will you know when you get there? When you have mined the Treasures to build your Little Red House and established your S.E.L.F. within it, how will you know?

Here's the key indicator: A S.E.L.F. consistently manufactures the fuel needed to enter the world of other people. This special fuel allows you to fill the tank of your C.A.R.—your Choice-Agency-Responsibility mobile. This three-wheeled vehicle carries you out of the safe home base of your Little Red House and into your relationships.

You will know you're living as your Self-governed, Ego-aware, Leading, and Free S.E.L.F. when, in every relationship you have, you:

- Know in your heart your life is created by your **choices**, and your loved one's life is created by her or his choices, and everyone else's lives are created by their choices.
- Clearly see your **agency** in life…and everyone else's agency. Agency is your ability to take action; agency initiates action, using your personal power. With agency, we live from the reality that each of us is an actor upon life, not its passive observer or victim.
- Acknowledge **responsibility** for your impact on your loved ones, invite everyone else in your life to acknowledge their impacts, and refuse to compromise on anyone's accountability for that impact, especially your own.

In the simplest terms, living as your S.E.L.F. means responsibly governing your life and staying the heck out of any efforts to govern anyone else's life. As the amazing Byron Katie puts it, "There's my business, your business, and God's business." She advises that all we must do is stay out of the latter two and focus on our choice of, agency in, and responsibility for the first.

My message is the best math equation ever: 7 + 3 = 1. Mine your *7 Childhood Treasures* to anchor the seven points of your Little Red House, mix up a batch of fuel for your three-wheeled C.A.R. for transport, and voila, you get one S.E.L.F. with the capacity to be in healthy relationship with others!

How can you tell if you're driving your Choice-Agency-Responsibility mobile out to meet others? Here are some indicators your forays into relationships are fueled by the right stuff.

Result #1: Your Life Is Your Choice

You'll know that you're living as your S.E.L.F. when you know, fully and deeply, that all of your life from now on is your choice. What you do, what you think, and how you feel are all within that realm of "it's my choice." Here are some key indicators you've achieved this result:

- You no longer say, "I had no choice," and become hyperaware of this language in the speech of others.
- You assess the choices available in each major opportunity or challenge in your life and select the option most in alignment with both your values and your goals.
- You no longer hear yourself blaming others or some vague "requirement" for your behavior, thoughts, or feelings. (As in, "I had to…," "She made me do it," "He makes me feel…," "She wouldn't let me," "He told me not to think like that," "I didn't want to get into trouble/piss her off/get him upset.") Again, hyperawareness of this language in the speech of others may be your clue to this change in your own thinking.
- You are able to give yourself an attitude adjustment. That is, when you find yourself suffering fear, grumpiness, anger, disappointment, or some other painful and unproductive emotion, you remind yourself you have the choice, then *make* the choice to feel differently, and do whatever is needed to shift gears emotionally.

This list is not exhaustive. There are certainly other indicators of this result of finding your S.E.L.F. As we explore the *Childhood Treasures* of Independence, Negotiation, and Vision, other indicators of this result will become evident.

Result #2: You Know You Have Agency

You'll know you're driving your C.A.R. with agency in your triple fuel when you turn to *yourself* as the first source of intervention in your own dissatisfactions. That is, you recognize your impact on yourself is greater than that of any other valued person, and you provide the *determining* impact on your own life. When you discover your dislike of a situation or circumstance in your life, you *begin* by looking for what *you* can do to create the change you want. You don't complain to, blame, or shame the people around you over your dissatisfaction. You reflect on your roles; you plan, alone or with others; you pray for divine guidance; or you take some other action.

When you live from the knowledge of your agency in the world:
- Defensiveness recedes. You no longer need to make excuses for, or even offer explanations for, your choices that do not harm others. When asked a simple informational question, such as "Did you turn off the lights?" you answer with a simple yes or no that carries no emotional energy. Period. You have no need to explain about why you didn't or did—unless someone asks for that explanation. (Please *do* apologize if you had committed to turning off the lights and didn't; offer to go do it now. Doing that without defensiveness or guilt is called accountability; see Result #3.)
- Codependency recedes. When declining an invitation to do something, such as "Do you want to go catch a movie?", you can graciously decline without explanation or manufactured excuse. Feeling no need to prevent or soothe hurt feelings you assume are occurring in the person inviting you, you hear yourself saying something simple like, "Oh, thank you so much for inviting me, but I'm going to pass. Enjoy the movie!" or "No thanks; maybe next time!" or "I think I'll stay home this time. Have fun!"
- Authenticity and honesty expand. No longer feeling it is your job to protect others from their own emotions, you simply relax and be who you are, within your values and from your belief that others are also self-governing in their lives. (Note that this does not give you license to act as you please and expect no consequences. If you are intentionally cruel, an emotional response is not only reasonable but appropriate.)
- You finally get rid of your "but." No more "I'd love to learn to fly a small plane BUT that's not going to happen!" or "I've always wanted to go to Ireland BUT I just don't have the money," or "I really need to get out of debt BUT I just don't see how." No more "She's the girl for me BUT she's way out of my league," or "I wanted to finish college BUT I never will." Instead, you hear yourself saying AND, adding "up to now," as in, "I'd love to learn to fly a small plane and, up to now, that hasn't happened," or "I wanted to finish college and, up to now, I haven't." Agency opens the door to endless possibilities.
- Positive outlook increases. You say "I can" and "I could" more often than "I can't" and "I should."

The **Childhood Treasures** of Faith and—surprisingly, perhaps—Compromise will help you achieve these and other indicators of Agency.

Result #3: You Take Responsibility

You are living as your S.E.L.F. when you are accountable for your words and deeds. Self-governance does not disregard others; your management of your life includes responsibly interacting with others. Some indicators of achieving this result of responsibility are:

- You are aware of the impact you have. Unlike the boat pilot who never looks back, you see your wake. You set intentions for the impact you want, such as "leaving more happiness everywhere I go." Then, you pay attention to the physical, auditory, emotional, and energetic impact you make on others. Different from the anxiety of worrying about your unknown future impact (i.e., worrying that you will "make" someone angry), this awareness is about being in the moment, moving toward your goal for the kind of impact you *want* to have, and noticing your *actual* impact now…and now…and now.
- Even when the impact you have on others—positive or negative—was not intentional, you can own the impact. You can take responsibility for the results of your choices without judging your choices, or yourself, as *bad* or *wrong*. If I share a fond memory of my mom and you cry because you just learned that your mom has a terminal condition that I didn't know about, my responsibility for your tears doesn't tell me that I shouldn't have shared my memory. Accountability in this circumstance means being there for you with empathy. Accountability also means being humbly grateful for our positive impacts on others, knowing that they do not make us better than others. By the way, your willingness to gracefully accept credit for positive impacts on others is a good model for how to be accountable for impacts that are less positive. Be just as humble and grateful.
- You do what you can to make amends for any unintended harm that results from your choices.

The **Childhood Treasures** of Trust, Independence, and Acceptance will help you build toward this result of responsibility.

There it is: the whole story. When gathered together, the *7 Childhood Treasures* make the home for your Self-governed, Ego-aware, Leading, Free S.E.L.F. Living from this safe home base, you create these three end results. In turn, they serve as the fuel that gets you to your relationship destinations in your Choice-Agency-Responsibility mobile, your C.A.R.

Now you are truly ready to begin the labor of digging up your buried birthright. Promised to you by your innate developmental programming, these gems still lie waiting as raw ores within you.

Your capacities for Trust, Independence, Faith, Negotiation, Vision, Compromise, and Acceptance are your best assets for a rich and productive life, full of purpose and joy. So, let's build that new home for your personality. Together, we're going to start systematically mining, refining, and polishing each of these gemstones.

Let's begin the journey…

The 7 Childhood Treasures and How They Grow

Everyone knows this one fact about child development: a child grows up. A child develops, transforms over time, and becomes…what? Each of us developed from a child to an adult, correct? Everyone knows that!

Actually, *maybe* is a more accurate answer. Some of us only developed partially. Some parts of us grew to adulthood, while others stayed young. Maybe only the body grew up and other capacities stayed as they were at age two, four, or six.

Dictionaries define "to develop" as growing into a more mature or advanced state. If we look at some of the people who walk around in adult bodies on reality TV shows, in our families and workplaces, or even in our government leadership, it would be hard to apply the words mature or advanced to their behavior. So, if many adults still act like children a great deal of the time, why do they?

Human development is easy to understand as a process, with just three components that are simple to define and tell apart from each other. In practice, however, the process is complex. Those components are designed for a careful, three-way balance, with well-timed windows of peak opportunity. The three components—maturation, learning, and construction—can work together. When this happy outcome occurs, it optimizes the intersection of nature (genetics) and nurture (environment) in each child.

Let's examine those three simple components. Some think of growing up as **maturation**, the inevitable unfolding of genetic seeds of potential. Do you believe a child develops as surely as a flower bud opens, as surely as a seed becomes a plant? You are one-third correct, and there are two more components that complement the maturation aspect of development.

Some think of development as **learning**, the gradual acquisition of skills, knowledge, and patterns of action and reaction. They, too, are one-third correct. The learning aspect of development results from external influences such as instruction, modeling, reward, and punishment. You tell a child a particular color is called red, ask her to repeat that word, and then praise her when she is correct. Voila! The modification of behavior and knowledge results in the component of development we call learning.

We're two-thirds of the way there. In addition to benefitting from these two passive processes, children are also agents in their own development. Remember Agency as part of the fuel in your C.A.R.? You had it from the start! You were an active participant in your development as a young child, and that's some really great news! Here's how you *know* you can be that active agent today: you were programmed for it from birth.

In addition to maturation and learning, your development required you to construct knowledge. From the raw materials available to you, you crafted comprehension, manufactured meaning, and sculpted significance. By raw materials, I mean the interactions you had with your physical and social world. Every relationship in your young life was a model for you to explore, a puzzle for you to solve, a piece of evidence for you to incorporate into your understanding of who you are and "how it goes" with others.

This is the third component of development: **construction**. You worked, both consciously and sub-consciously, to make sense of what happened to you, every moment of every day. You used your interactions with the social world as tools to shape your sense of identity. Like the tools for mining actual gems, these interactions with other humans were your pickaxes, shovels, grinding stones, and polishers for the construction of a reality. You *constructed* your beliefs about who you are as a person and who other people are to you. You crafted your own understanding of the social world in which you lived, and you wrote your own rules about how to get along in that world. Regardless of whether you remember this construction process, you engaged in it daily. All children do. In fact, we still do it as adults.

To better understand construction as a development process, let's see what construction looks like in another area of development. Children also develop scientific and mathematical knowledge through construction, along with direct learning from books, the Internet, and teachers. Here's how the construction part works:

When children act upon the physical world, and it reacts in certain ways, they construct ideas about how the world works. As the physical world is so much less complicated than the social world, a toddler learning physics makes an easier example as a metaphor for construction of social knowledge:

As she searches for a favorite book her mother has promised to read before her nap, twenty-two-month-old Miranda pulls a small car out of her toy box. She drops the car, and it lands by chance on the lid to the toy box, which is resting against the side of the box at a slant of about forty-five degrees to the floor. The car lands on its wheels, rolls swiftly to the floor, and then continues for about three feet more across the floor. Miranda is captured by the sound of the rolling car and stops her search, watching the car's final inches of descent down the lid and its roll across the floor. When it comes to rest, she grunts a startled "Huh!" and toddles over to retrieve the car. Back at the toy box, she places it on the tilted lid and releases it.

Ten minutes later, her mother arrives in the doorway, wondering why Miranda is taking so long to get the book, and finds her daughter releasing the car at the top of the ramp for what is, unbeknownst to mom, the sixteenth time. In the intervening ten minutes, Miranda has released the car at the top, middle, and bottom of the ramped lid, has released it on its back and on its wheels, front hood first, back trunk first, and sideways, in varying combinations, over and over and over, each time watching how far it rolls or slides before coming to rest.

Miranda, on this random afternoon of her young life, was constructing some of her earliest knowledge of physics. She built that knowledge, bit by bit, through a process of self-directed discovery. She acted on the environment and observed the results. She could not yet articulate the physics principles involved in her "play." Indeed, at that age she could barely say "the car rolls" and be understood by someone other than her parents. But on that day, she constructed an early glimmer of new understanding about the physical world and how it works.

Children construct knowledge of the social world in the same way. Just as Miranda acted on the car, children "act on" (that is, interact with) other humans, observe the outcomes, and figure out what it all means. When you were an infant, toddler, preschooler, and young child, each interaction you had with another person provided you with tools. With those tools, you transformed the genetically provided raw materials within you. You actively built components of your self—your personality and identity—based on these interactions with your social world.

In addition to noticing what happens when they act on their social worlds, children also observe how other humans act on/interact with each other. Adult lives are like a stage play that children watch and interpret. For example:

Carmine, with his fourth birthday just weeks behind him, sits at the dinner table and listens to his parents argue. Momma is, at first, firm and strong-voiced, then more tense and jittery as she insists she needs more money for the household budget. Poppa is yelling and swearing a lot, waving his big arms in the air while holding his fork. "No way!" he hollers. "Marie, I tell ya, you can't get blood out of a turnip!" he yells, as the fist holding his fork bangs the table and a piece of hamburger flies off onto the floor. Momma quiets and says in a soothing voice, "Okay, Johnny, okay; whatever you say. I'll make do."

The next day at lunch, when Momma tells Carmine to finish his carrots, he waves one slice wildly on his fork until it flies across the room and, banging both fists on the table, yells, "No way! I tell ya, you got blood in this carrot!" Momma swats the fork from his hand, pulls him roughly from his chair, and drops him into his time-out chair, saying, "Don't you say no to me, young man! Wait till your poppa hears about this! Blood in the carrots. Hmph! Blasphemy!"

Miranda observed sixteen repeated trials of her physics experiment with the car and the toy box lid. Carmine appears to have needed just one example of his parent's social dynamic to construct his somewhat off-target version of this pattern. More likely, Momma Marie and Poppa Johnny have regular fights in which Marie asserts herself, then backs off and becomes conciliatory in the face of Johnny's yelling and large gestures. Carmine has probably witnessed this pattern many times in his four years of life. Perhaps throwing his carrot off his fork at lunch was not even the first time he has imitated his father's tantrums.

Has Carmine been punished consistently for these mock fights with Momma? Do they sometimes go unnoticed, or are some of his Poppa-like incidents rewarded by Poppa's laughter? *Whatever* happens, Carmine uses each and every interaction with his parents to build his knowledge of how mommas and poppas interact, how men and women negotiate. In fact, he is polishing up an overall understanding of how men behave and how women behave. He is constructing a social understanding of gender differences in power and communication. He's constructing concepts about appropriate emotional expression and communication strategies, how to behave in a negotiation—and so much more.

This construction process is the third component of human development. Maturation brings windows of opportunity, while construction creates unique understanding and points of view. Learning brings us the skills to express those understandings and points of view, as well as the ability to understand the broader contexts related to them.

The intricate braiding of these three components of development is the process that enables us to mine and gather the ***7 Childhood Treasures*** between birth and seven years of age. Maturation made you ready to mine one of these gems in each of your first seven years. Learning gave you some of the skills you needed to take advantage of these seven windows of opportunity. Then the adults in your life, and maybe some older children, gave you the social construction tools enabling you to unearth and claim these treasures, or they did not. Most likely, they did not.

Like Carmine, you compiled these treasures as best you could, to be the anchor bolts for your Little Red House, your home for who you are as a social and emotional being, as an "inter-actor" with others. You could only mine using the tools the world gave you. Each exchange with a parent, another family member, a child care teacher, or a neighbor left you holding the instruments with which to excavate the dark ores that were intended as the glittering gems to anchor your home for a S.E.L.F. If all went well, you got the sturdy pickaxes, grinding stones, and polishing cloths needed for the job. You have claimed your birthright of emotional health and intelligence and embedded it into your safe home of personality, which we're imagining as your Little Red House.

If all went well, you govern your own life and stay out of others' business, unless invited in. You are aware of your mind's conversation with itself and know how to get a wider perspective. You are a leader in your life, and your leadership focuses on freedom from self-imposed barriers. You live from awareness of your choices, act from knowledge of your agency, and take responsibility for your impact on others.

If it all went that well, you would be reading something else right now.

If the folks in your social world—no matter how well-intentioned—kept handing you shoddy tools, bent picks, and dull axes, you may still struggle to find your Self-governed, Ego-aware, Leading, and Free S.E.L.F. Maybe, at age seven, you were holding only a partial pile of nuggets, still raw ores, awaiting refinement. If that's the case, then we'll be digging and polishing soon!

First, for what are we mining?

What is Trust?

The first psychosocial lesson of life for all of us is that we must trust others to meet our needs. I know. I hate needing too. However, we humans are pack animals, interdependent. So, yes, we must trust others to meet some of our needs.

The vulnerability of infancy is specially designed to allow us to learn that lesson. A newborn child is utterly dependent. If there are not others of his species there to keep him alive, he will die. This complete and desperate dependence is a state of being that we adults are rarely, if ever, interested in experiencing. Yet that is the way all of us entered the world, and it is the way many of us will leave it.

In between, a lot of us try not to depend on anyone other than ourselves, or we depend entirely on one person for every need. Neither is a sustainable alternative to Trust, derived as a ***Childhood Treasure***.

Remember for a moment holding a newborn infant, or if you've not had the experience, imagine what a newborn infant is like. Hold out your two hands and feel her; see her held there in front of you. She is tiny. Just six or seven pounds, a little heavier than a bag of sugar or a two-liter bottle of soda pop, a little lighter than a gallon of water or milk. Both the shoulders and seemingly outsized head fit into one of your hands. Inside this little wriggly, randomly moving bundle of flesh and muscle, you know there are small, soft bones. Your other hand feels the firmness of a pelvis so small that the span from your thumb to baby finger may wrap all the way around those tiny hips and up the sides of the waist.

It's scary for you to hold her out in the air like that because her random and jerky movements make her an unpredictable package. She also feels insecure out there away from you, so her wriggling intensifies, and she begins to squeak a bit or squall out her need for safety. On this—her first day of life—her cry is thin, reedy, shaky.

Instinctively, you pull her in, folding your arms around her and pressing her entire front to your chest. She feels the full-body support to which she has been accustomed these past nine months, floating in a big bag of warm fluid within her birth mother's comfortably heated torso.

With this soothing contact, neurochemicals surge across several hundred million open spaces in her little brain and are instantly followed by a jolt of electricity that forms a bridge across what was an open space. Hundreds of millions of neurons have fired together, for the first time, and continue to fire over and over every second that you hold this infant and meet her need for security. (Your neurons are firing too, along pathways of love, connection, and empathy built in your first few years of life.)

In these moments of holding close, you are giving this child a tool she needs to mine her first Childhood Treasure: Trust. She has taken that tool—the relief of having a physical need met—and begun a process that can lead her into healthy trust in her future relationships.

These same new brain connections will respond again and again to hundreds of thousands of such moments. Every time this new babe feels hungry, tired, ready to play, or physically uncomfortable, and some caregiver comes and relieves that need, her growing brain fires across those same bridges of connection. Every experience of need felt/need met strengthens a neural network around this baby's certainty that the world has her back.

Think of that web of connections in the brain as another tool you are giving this baby for her mining of the Treasure of Trust. She is learning whether she can depend on others in her environment to respond to her expressions of need and to fulfill those needs. When you were a newborn, also so tiny that you fit into two cupped hands, you learned this too.

What if you experienced a different pattern? What if sometimes—or many times—you felt a need for security and that need was not met? Parents and other caregivers often don't know a lot about taking care of infants. They get an array of advice from many, many sources, some of which conflicts, and some of which is flat-out poor guidance, not well-grounded in our current understanding of brain development and the impact of early experience.

When I was a newborn in the mid-1950s, the advice of the moment was from Dr. Benjamin Spock. One of the key features of parenting advice back then was to use scheduled feeding and naps. Never mind that your newborn is crying to be fed or picked up and held *right now*; it's not time for a bottle, baby dearest. Feeding your baby on *his* hunger schedule or letting him sleep and wake to *his* internal rhythms was seen as how you "spoiled" a child. We know now that this point of view is outdated. In fact, it is based on adult projections of meaning onto infant behavior. Infants can't be spoiled by caregiving that responds to their needs.

When babies cry, they are not complaining or manipulating, they are communicating. Crying is one of the few forms of language they have at first. The caregiver's job is to learn that language, to learn how to interpret the child's actual meaning rather than presuming adult motivations are behind infant behavior. A crying infant is not pressuring you or being willful; she's just hungry.

Imagine this: Baby lies in her crib, screaming at the top of her little lungs, what she knows as this message: "I NEED YOU! HELP! I NEED YOU!" What if nobody comes? What if nobody relieves the sharp emptiness that chews on her from the inside like a beast? What if nobody takes away the cold wetness that chafes her tender skin? What if nobody comes to let her know that she is not alone, feeling that she is dying for lack of your sheltering arms?

I'll tell you what happens: she stops crying after a while. It's the most heartbreaking thing in the world to watch. At first, she tries to comfort herself, to meet her own need. She'll cry again in a little while but with less force and for less time. This also happens: she stops believing her needs will be met. She stops believing anyone cares what she needs.

Many parents may not know that *every* interaction with a young child fires up hundreds of millions of new connections in their newborn's brain, literally constructing 90 percent of brain architecture by five years of age. Just because a parent or other caregiver isn't there doesn't mean there's no interaction happening; it doesn't mean there are no neurons forming connections. That crying baby is interacting with a scary and lonely world, the World Where Nobody Cares. What neurons are firing and wiring together as this little babe cries, alone and hungry, cold, or frightened?

I assure you those experiences don't build the same neural network as when an infant's physical needs are consistently relieved. But they do, indeed, build a brain's basic infrastructure.

This child is not receiving the tools to mine the Treasure of Trust. The raw ore from which she could be mining her capacity for Trust is being buried more deeply with each passing moment of needing in which her needs are not met.

So, what is Trust? In the end, Trust, for us adults, is a willingness to depend on others to meet some of our needs. Trust is vulnerability; it is allowing ourselves to need other people. Trust is knowing that it's safe to need people *because they will be there for you*. If you have Trust, you can feel safe when you need something and depend on someone else to meet that need. With the Treasure of Trust, you know that the world has your back.

What is Independence?

As you mine your first Treasure, Trust, you gain the important tool of knowing your body is separate from the rest of the world, including separate from other people's bodies. Your understanding of your *physical boundary* (your skin), which contains all the physical parts of you, is born from that dance between feeling a need and having that need relieved. We each began to understand, right around three months of age, that there is a ME who feels the hunger, the need, and there is an OTHER who comes to relieve it. This rudimentary understanding of physical two-ness—the self and the other—is the beginning of the *nonphysical boundaries* that enable us to mine Independence.

I use this term *boundaries* in the sense that clinical psychologists mean it, not in the common usage, as in, "I set a boundary: I told him he couldn't XYZ anymore." In **7 Childhood Treasures** lingo, that kind of statement is not a boundary but a *limit*. Learning to set limits is part of mining the Treasure of Negotiation, which happens a few years farther down the developmental path.

First, before being able to set limits, which is an intentional act of agency, we must learn that we *own ourselves* inside some clearly defined perimeters: the edges of ourselves. That's a key feature of boundaries that differentiates them from limits: We don't set boundaries; we either own them or we don't.

Think of boundaries as the containers of yourself, like a banana peel contains the banana. Boundaries are the sides or edges or walls of a container, like that physical boundary of skin that holds in all your muscles, organs, bones, and a whole lot of water.

As a toddler, coming into your second year of life, you began to build upon what you learned about your body's boundary of skin. At that time, we hope you added a boundary of mind or intellect, a boundary of heart or emotion, and a boundary of yearning or dreams longed for. We'll shorthand that last one as the boundary of soul. Let's think of each as a simple brown paper bag. When we come out of the toddler year and head into the first of the preschool years, we need to know not only that we have a skin bag, but also an "emotions bag," a "thoughts bag," and a "bag of soul."

How do we see these boundaries emerging in the young child? Have you ever been in a room full of toddlers? It's an experience everyone should have once! In many states, a roomful (defined by child care licensing rules) is twelve to sixteen: twelve to sixteen children between about eighteen and thirty months, supervised by two adults. The fundamental challenge for the adults in this roomful of toddlers is that no one in the room (except, we hope, the adults) knows who they are and who they are not.

Younger toddlers own none of their boundaries yet, other than their skin sacks. For example, without a thoughts sack (mental boundary), they believe whatever *they* think, know, or remember is also thought, known, or remembered by *you*. Whatever memories they have of last night, when you weren't together, will be assumed to be your memories too.

With no emotions sack/boundary, whatever they feel, emotionally, they believe you feel it right along with them, and vice versa! Whatever feeling is expressed spreads quickly in a toddler room—emotions are contagious when you don't have a sack to hold your feelings together.

Without a boundary/sack of soul, whatever a toddler wants, he is sure that *you want it for him* just as much as he wants it for himself. With no boundary on his yearnings or his dreams, a toddler cannot conceive that someone else could *not* want him to have what he wants. Even farther from toddlers' understanding is the notion that others might also want what they want but for themselves, and that could lead to conflict!

When adults in the lives of toddlers know how to help them develop these boundaries of mind, heart, and soul, they hand them mining tools such as mirrors to look in, names for the feelings they are having, strategies for expressing them, descriptions of how others are feeling, and explanations about why they are experiencing those emotions. Helpful adults give toddlers opportunities to express their thoughts and take them seriously. Children who successfully mine the Treasure of Independence are handed opportunities to reflect on what they want and to practice their "choice muscle," making and remaking little toddler-sized decisions.

Unfortunately for many of our former toddler selves, the prevailing parenting style in American households has long echoed a nineteenth-century mindset that classified these beings with no boundaries, these semi-wild little humans as contrary, difficult, even terrible in their two-ness. The goal of parenting toddlers, for more than 150 years now, has been to break their will.

Toddlers' wanting of things, around which there is no boundary yet—their ways of pushing their points of view and the tidal waves of emotion that they use to drive their little agendas—these preprogrammed developmental traits are too often judged negatively by adult standards. We see toddlers as willful and inconsiderate little beasties who must be tamed. Doubt me? Just listen sometime to the ways parents and toddler teachers talk about their toddlers.

Perhaps, just as you were needing to learn that you have boundaries—that you are unique and valuable—you instead learned that you were wrong, and in many ways. You were likely told that you should not feel your wild and unbridled feelings. You should not try to make others do what you want. You should not say those words.

My favorite, when I worked in preschools, was teachers who told young ones what they needed, as in, "You need to stop running and come sit down." Yeah…not really. If these kids had the verbal prowess I have, I imagine them saying, "Actually, I need to run! And you can tell that's what I need because that's what I'm doing. Now, I hear that YOU need me to stop running and come sit down, but that's not really what I need."

In such moments, boundaries are born and can be nurtured. If the teacher can own her own boundary of soul and stop projecting what she wants onto that little whirling dervish who has completely different wants in this moment, we might all get somewhere with mining the Treasure of Independence!

I pause here to acknowledge that, along with masses of joy, there is continuous pain and sadness in parenting, often first felt by parents when their child is at this age. The lifetime of a child is one long process of individuation, of gradually separating from the parenting adults and other authorities. With each developmental stage, children find new ways of saying, "I am me. I am NOT you!" to their parents. That's the source of the grief of parenting; for the children, there is only the joy of becoming who they are meant to be—a unique, Self-governed, Ego-aware, Leading, Free S.E.L.F.!

Parents who have mined their own Independence navigate this loss better because Independence is knowing who you are and who you are not. Boundaries bring the inexplicable bliss of finding those pleasant places where the edges of you can find harmony, lined up along the edges of others. The Treasure of Independence is polished bright and shining in the foundation of your Little Red House when you have boundaries of body, mind, heart, and soul *in the context of relationships*. Knowing the edges of who you are and seeing the edges of others is only valuable if you're actually *relating* with those others, exchanging ideas, sharing feelings, planning, and dreaming together.

We can't learn that each of us has ideas, beliefs, dreams, and emotional responses in common or in sympathy if I don't know what mine are and you don't know yours. If I can't find the edges of who I *am*, differentiating it from who I am *not*, then I might still be like that boundary-less toddler, catching the contagion of whatever you think, feel, or want.

Without the Treasure of Independence, I'm a creature in constant metamorphosis or mutation, adopting and adapting to the thoughts, beliefs, feelings, and dreams of whomever is around. With Independence, I am I, and I have *relationships* with others: friends, family, and other loved ones. I relate with others rather than merging with them. I experience others rather than managing them.

What is Faith?

Faith is the dream that will not die. It is belief in all that we imagine, or fear, may be impossible: belief in magic, God, fairies, life beyond the death of the body, as well as our dreams of making a difference, of making our mark on the world. Faith is our awe at the beauty of our world and the wider universe, and our passion to live our own lives fully and authentically. Faith is the **Childhood Treasure** of the three-year-old.

By the time you were approaching this age, you had been focused for more than two years on your own little self. Egocentrism—knowing with absolute certainty that you're the center of the universe—is the hallmark of these first two years, as it should be. First, you spent some time discovering your body, then you labored to discover your opinions, feelings, and dreams. You would be so proud if you could travel back in time and watch your efforts at that age! Assuming you were handed all the right mining tools for Trust and Independence, here's what you'd see:

There she is, owning her whole self, expressing what she thinks with confidence that her voice has unique value in every conversation. Watch as she feels passion for her life and also compassion for others. Notice how her emotions flow freely within her and are expressed in ways that deepen emotional intimacy and strengthen relationships. Yes, at three years old!

A child of this age still speaks—usually loudly enough for everyone within twenty feet to hear—the absolute "truth" of whatever he observes. "Why is that man bald?" "Why is that woman in a chair with wheels?" "Wow, she is SO fat!" See how he also speaks the truth about whatever he wants, confident that life is an abundant smorgasbord? Yet, you can see that he also knows that a "no" doesn't change his value as a person or render his desire irrelevant. This self-contained little child is happily living in the interior world he has discovered as ME.

As you watch in your imagination, this almost-three-year-old suddenly lifts his gaze from this two-year-old focus on his own navel. It's almost as if, in one magical moment, he discovers the wider world around him. He notices the rest of the universe, of which he is now only *pretty* sure he is the center. "Oh, wow. My goodness! Look at that! And look at THAT! And THAT!!"

And, suddenly, three-ness is off and running. Threes are amazed by nearly everything they see, hear, and feel. Each experience is a rhapsody of wonder. The world is a magical place when you live outside the world of logic, which this age child still does. This is the age at which you literally believe that everything, *anything*, is possible.

Be the first boy to grow up to be a mommy, stop people from dying from diseases like cancer, create a language that lets us talk with other animals…. At this age, children see no limits to their desires, their longings. They have Big Dreams, dreams that will take a lifetime or more to live into being, and they have perfect Faith that those dreams will live. Big Dreams are the hallmark of the Treasure of Faith.

Let me give you an ancient example of a Big Dream. I once had the delightful experience of a visit to the restored site of a Neolithic village called New Grange in Ireland. A short drive from Dublin, this cluster of stone buildings sits at the top of a high point from which you can survey many miles. Just below, a small river winds, nestled below the curve of this emerald hilltop. At the center of this site is a temple to the summer solstice sun. Constructed entirely of stone, without the use of any metal tools, this circular building has a domed roof made from slabs of stone lain in increasingly smaller circles. The center space is covered by a capstone. As you follow the tour guide through an open doorway, she points out a rectangular opening above the door frame.

On three days each year, the summer solstice sun shines through that opening at dawn and floods the interior chamber with golden light. A small tribe with no metal tools and a Stone Age understanding of the solar system conceived of and built this miracle of architecture. Here comes the Big Dream part of the story: The tour guide said that archaeologists estimate it took three generations of workers to build this temple. Three generations!

That's how Big Dreams work. One person conceived of and calculated the design for this solstice temple at New Grange then engaged the whole tribe in the passionate vision and worked the rest of her life on the construction. Life spans were much shorter then, so let's say she gave ten years to her Big Dream. Those ten years inspired the next generation to make her dream their own, and they spent most of their whole twenty or thirty years on its construction, only to die with it still unfinished. Then the grandchildren of the original designer's generation finished it.

That's the kind of inspiration-filled life that comes from the Treasure of Faith. We each have a special something, a unique purpose, to fulfill in this life. For some, it is the building of temples or the making of art; for some, it is being a loving parent who rears whole, healthy, inspired children who achieve their Big Dreams. For some, it is saving whales who become stranded on a beach, and for others, it is offering a smile and a cheery greeting to every customer served. Whether your Big Dream raises a roof or a child, saves a life or graces a moment in a life, whether you change the world or change one corner of it, Faith is what leads you to do whatever senseless acts of beauty, kindness, innovation, and inspiration you commit in this world.

Faith is the passion for life that gets you out of bed every morning. Faith gives you the strength to keep going when circumstances seem to overwhelm you with barriers. Faith is the heart that beats the pulse of your purpose, keeping energy flowing through you like a mighty river. Your unique greatness may not be of the kind that gets your picture on the covers of magazines, but whatever your greatness, it is uniquely yours, and the world would be less if you failed to pursue it.

To know *that* truth is to know you have fully mined and polished the **Childhood Treasure** of Faith.

Families that foster Faith are ones in which these Big Dreams of little children are respected. The fanciful ideas of threes are not for our entertainment. Laughter and comments of "How adorable!" or "Wow! That's a doozy!" are completely inappropriate, just as they would be if we were responding to a coworker's innovative idea. Faith-mining tools are simple once we remove our core assumption of incompetence from young children.

The first big pickaxe is the ability to honor the amazing creativity and productivity of three-year-olds while dropping our judgment of the absence of even basic logic (still far in this kid's future, at around age six or seven). No matter how wild the idea, how far beyond the adult's understanding of what is possible, the response of, "Yes, let's try that," is the tool that unfailingly opens the seam of this raw ore.

What is Negotiation?

Keep thinking of that three-year-old for a moment. Arms stretched wide, running at the world on tiptoe with a squeal of glee, he sees everything with new and innocent eyes. He consumes it all and loves it all, takes every encounter at its face value, believes in the magic of every moment, and is simply and continuously awed by life. Threes swim, fully immersed, in life, with a sense of luxurious openness to every experience their senses bring them.

Then they turn four. Those wide-open arms are quickly crossed and locked over their little rib cages, and suddenly, it's all about the rules, the law, and being right. Oh, and fair. From the open and willing "I BELIEVE!" stance of the three-year-old, the four-year-old shape-shifts into a little Missouri mule, four feet squarely planted, saying, "Show me."

The pattern of these shifts from toddler to three to four is an eloquent illustration of the nature of child development as a process. The journey of individuation is not a direct straight line outward, moving ever farther away from the bond with parents. This developmental "pathway" is really more of a pulsing, out and back, out and back. Children move away from the home-base security of connection with a family, then return for a safety check, then move outward again a little farther this time, and a little farther the time after that. And they always return, even up to the death of the parent and beyond. Most of us still reference our parents' counsel even when their advice lives only in our memory.

The age of four is one of those times when we came back to the security of adult approval, returning from the outer stratosphere of Big Dreaming. At four, you wanted nothing more than to learn how your edges fit up against everyone else's. Preferably very tidily. Now is when those boundaries, mined as the Treasure of Independence, become fully understood and essential. At four, you first saw your boundaries' real purpose from a higher level of understanding. This is when boundaries become the source from which we set limits and make agreements in relationships.

This is the age at which you learn to cope with the fact that other people have agendas different from your own. If all has gone well so far, you know who you are—what you think, feel, and want—and you understand that others have thoughts, feelings, and desires different from your own. This is the age at which you learn how to operate, day-to-day, within that reality. At four, you start to learn how to *understand* others' interests that differ from your own and create win-win solutions when your interests conflict with others.

Fours have two driving imperatives: 1) figure out how to get what I want within the context of what others want; and 2) do that by figuring out the rules of every social/interpersonal "game." Maybe that game is "Me and Mommy Deciding What's for Lunch," or "Getting to Wear My Superman Cape to Church." Social games for the four-year-old mind are pretty simple because they're only trying to meet a basic need for self-determination. For many of us adults, that navigation task has become quite complex, but that's only because we didn't get enough help with mining the Treasure of Negotiation when we were four.

Negotiation looks for the win-win solution. When you were four, you were striving to be a little diplomat. You were a budding negotiator in your family and in the other social circles of your life—maybe a neighborhood cluster of kids, maybe a preschool classroom. Though not consciously, you spent most of your time assessing the limits set by others and figuring out where your interests fit inside those limits.

Imagine for a moment that you're a four playing the "Deciding What's for Lunch" game with Mom. If Mom was knocking her role out of the park, she opened the game by offering you a choice between two lunch options, both of which were inside her set of limits for the game. We can envision Mom's limits—the expression of her interests as a parent—as if they are the sides of a cube.

One side limits the options to what she considers appropriate nutrition for lunch today, which is balanced by her knowledge of the breakfast and snacks eaten so far and what is planned for later in the day. Another side of the cube is likely that the ingredients need to be available in the house; she's not going shopping to make lunch happen. A third side might be ease of preparation because of other demands on her time at midday. Sides four, five, and six of this cube—a box, if you will—could include a variety of other limits, such as allergies you or she have, knowledge of your food preferences and dislikes, previously experienced food battlegrounds, your current general health, or some specific dental health issue of the moment. So many possible sides to this one little box that contains the options for lunch!

When this game goes well, Mom's roles are: 1) knowing that she *has* a "box" of limits and what those limits are, and 2) offering a couple of options that fit inside all of her limits. Your role, as the child in the game, is to get the lunch you want using the same box of limits—only you may not yet fully understand what all of them are. For the child, part of the game is to *learn* about them.

Fours are learning, through efforts at negotiation, to assess the sides of the Negotiation boxes in which they find themselves placed by adults. Fours are (or should be) put into hundreds of such boxes every day, maybe more. Boxes of reasonable, consciously set limits provide for the protection of the child's health and safety, for the rearing of the child according to specific values and beliefs, for the learning of societal conventions for behavior that are shared within a culture, and more.

If adults are playing these "social games" with intention and awareness, they are handing over every tool the child needs to mine and polish his Treasure of Negotiation. Every time a four-year-old finds herself in one of these "Negotiation boxes," she makes her move in the negotiation game. She may offer an alternative, striving to balance her desire to make it *different* from those offered by the adult, yet also a fit inside the adult's parameters as she understands them. If Mom offers a choice of tuna salad on whole wheat or stuffed into a tomato, maybe the child will negotiate for a BLT because she knows Dad had bacon for breakfast and there is *always* lettuce. Let's assume that this alternative is targeted to be within Mom's limits that all 1) ingredients are available and 2) meets nutrition expectations for the meal and day.

When the child shoots this hopeful arrow of a proposed third option into what she believes is the interior of Mom's Negotiation box, she learns how to do it better the next time. That occurs *if* Mom and other adults in her life played the game with the goal of helping her develop Negotiation skills. Some adults—especially those who didn't mine their own Treasure of Negotiation—squelch, rather than support, these efforts.

Their kind of my-way-or-the-highway parenting requires children to follow explicit and unilateral decisions on what they wear and eat, who they play with and befriend, and how they behave in pretty much every situation. If you grew up under one of these authoritarian regimes at home or school, you know how quickly that boot on your neck starts to chafe your spirit. Resistance, and eventually defiance, is among the obvious courses for these children.

We are *supposed* to be able to negotiate for what we want as adults. The diplomatic skills to create win-win solutions are valuable assets in the workplace and in our personal lives. Four years of age, with our hands on our hips, eyes narrowed, as we watch others to figure out all the rules—that is when we are designed, by nature, to claim this Treasure.

What is Vision?

That pulsing process of individuation that I described on p. 31 continues. We move away, come back, explore, return. The process that brought us closer to parents, rules, and the interiors of Negotiation boxes at four years of age now opens outward again as we approach five years. This outward pulse at five years of age is where we explode into achievement, or don't. The **Childhood Treasure** of Vision calls to us, like a siren's song, urging us to reach for attainable goals with specific plans. At five years, before we hit kindergarten, we become the little strategic planners of the childhood world.

Five-year-olds have acquired a double fistful of skills enabling this emergence of the Planner. Muscles in the face have matured enough to ensure well-articulated speech. That gives everyone around him access to his thoughts, beliefs, and feelings, all of which are in plentiful supply. From the immature speech of the almost three-year-old—understood by family members only half the time and by almost nobody else the rest of the time—he has grown into a natural speaker of his native tongue by five.

Assuming she is in an environment that is language-rich, her vocabulary is skyrocketing into tens of thousands of words. By the age of four-and-a-half, children usually prefer to start the day talking and, pretty much, never stop unless they put food in their mouths or fall asleep. Uninterrupted, healthy kids this age can actually achieve this goal!

The neural network of the brain is also achieving its peak at this age. Since birth, 90 percent of the brain has been literally constructed, built for the first time, connection by connection. In fact, children have more neural connections at five than they will ever have again! The computing power of this network can be phenomenal, and fives get pretty busy with their plans to run the world according to their Vision.

Different from the impossible, magical Big Dreams you dreamed at three years, your Big Ideas at five were for more "achievable" projects. At three, you saw how you wanted to change the way the world worked, and so you dreamed dreams that might take several lifetimes to realize. At five, you wanted to explore the world as it is and, you know, maybe *tinker* with it a bit. At this age, right on the cusp of transitioning to kindergarten, you were a popcorn-popper of ideas that could, mostly, be accomplished within a few minutes, hours, or months.

Have you ever watched a group of five-year-olds playing? Their brainstorming and planning aptitudes are easy to observe. As a young preschool director, I witnessed the exercise of these planning muscles every day. My mixed-age groups of threes, fours, and fives and I lived together in the mid-1980s era of the first three Star Wars movies (episodes IV, V, and VI, for those who care), and every day the five-year-old kids huddled up at the beginning of our thirty-minute outdoor play time to plan their Star Wars play. Every day, they assigned roles ("I'll be Han Solo and you be Luke, okay?"), mapped out plot points ("First, we'll hyperjump in the Millennium Falcon to the fourth moon of Endor, then we'll blow up the power generator, right?"), and set up the dramatic moments ("Wait, wait! Then Darth Vader comes out the door, okay?").

So happy and contented were they with their exercise of Vision that, most days, they planned and planned and planned how to play Star Wars for the whole half-hour. Their parents arrived and, one by one, pulled them out of the little strategy huddle and into a car until they were all gone for the day.

The next day, they'd pour through the door onto the playground, huddle up, and plan all over again: the same role assignments, sketching out plot points, and preblocking of dramatic moments. Every day, planning but no playing.

Back when you were five, you exercised your brainstorming and planning skills all the time. You probably popped out a few hundred ideas a week for exciting things to do, places to go, and things to build. That is, if the adults in your life were handing you the tools you needed for this mining of the Treasure of Vision. Many parents unintentionally step on their children's visions because they don't know how to help them.

What do you say to a five-year-old child who wants to build a rocket to the moon, or invent a way to clean up the water in the nearby stream, or use Legos to build a scale replica of the White House on the front lawn? Such Big Ideas are too often met with, if not outright mocking, or gentle amusement, then more compassionate messages such as, "You can't do that, honey, you're just a little kid." If adults were being fully honest, we would probably say, "Wow! What a great idea! I haven't a clue how to help you do that!"

When adults can see and be at least a little bit open to the genius of the fives in their lives, then they can say yes to any Big Idea. Here's why: All attempts to achieve a Big Idea are chock-full of great learning, fun, and community building, even if the goal is not achieved. If parents and teachers can say, "Let's try that! What should we do first?" then they will quickly learn that every planning process and every implementation *effort* has value beyond measure.

In exploration of a path to a goal, through trial after trial and error after error, children learn to reason, read, measure, calculate, research, rethink, and recalculate. Most valuable of all, they learn that errors can improve implementation. This is the age at which children can learn, like Thomas Edison, that there are a thousand or more ways *not* to do something like invent a light bulb, and that each of those ways teaches us some new thing about how we *can* achieve our vision. Five is the age when we develop the habit of perseverance.

Vision is the ***Childhood Treasure*** that keeps us intellectually interested in life for decades. It's the capacity that leads us to invent tools—from the simplicity of picking up a stick to fish out something we dropped in a creek to the complexity of robotic arms that assemble other tools, like cars, for us to use. Vision is the Treasure that makes fives ask "Why?" and "How?" and "What if?" all day long.

If we had the adult support we needed to mine and cut and polish this gemstone, then we still approach life from that place of open curiosity. We identify something as a problem, barrier, or less-than-desirable situation and we think of ways to fix it, make it better, or solve it. Because of Vision, a tiny baby rabbit with no hind legs gets to move around with its front legs while its body is encased in a little sock secured to a mini-skateboard. Because of Vision, a soldier whose legs were taken by the inventions of war can run and jump on artificial legs with microcomputer processors built into the joints. Because of Vision, we put men on the moon, a computerized dune buggy on Mars, and a telescope far beyond the edges of our solar system to send us photos of the universe.

With Vision fully mined, cut, and polished, each of us can become the maker of our own way, the solver of our own problems, and the designer of our own world. You'll not only set substantial goals and achieve them, you may become a phenomenal inventor of life hacks!

What is Compromise?

The pulsing respiration of individuation—leaving home base security for the unknown and then hustling back—never really stops. We do continue to return to our home bases throughout our lives. That said, this exhaling expansion that began at five continues at six, pulsing outward and farther outward for many years, with fewer and fewer returns to home base. Those returns also evolve, becoming more and more subtle, even as they become more infrequent.

By the teen years, a momentary flash of a smile and eye contact gets tallied in the "return to home base" category, even if the teen is across the country, connecting by FaceTime.

This big push outward at six parallels the advent of "formal" schooling in America and early logic in the young child. As we transition from five to six years of age, we move from a contained little world in which we are the chief goal setter/planner to an open-ended, multilayered, and somewhat unpredictable world called kindergarten. It is this new venue that provides the impetus to mine the **Childhood Treasure** of Compromise. I invite you to remember or imagine the changes inherent in this year of transition from the point of view of that child.

So, there you were in your year before kindergarten. Remember? No? Then imagine. Children this age are usually at home or in some form of child care or preschool the year before they enter kindergarten. Maybe you spent most of your day playing or engaging with learning materials that interested you, with lots of choices for activities that you self-directed. Maybe you spent too much of it watching television. Maybe you spent time outside in the woods or with animals.

Depending on the size of your family or the type of early education and care setting you were in, you shared a supervising, caring adult either not at all, as an only child, or with nine or so others in a family child care setting (usually a woman offering child care in her home, known to the unschooled as a "babysitter"). Maybe the group you were in was just you and a parent or grandparent. Maybe it was as large as twenty or twenty-five in a Pre-K classroom.

That was the last year and the year before. Now, here it is the opening day of kindergarten, and you're sharing one supervising, caring adult with thirty or forty other children, depending on how badly underfunded your public school classrooms are.

This new environment is full of confusing, even nonsensical, activities and events. A voice comes out of nowhere announcing events you don't understand, reciting a sing-songy "pledge" with mysterious words you can't quite make out ("Did she say God is invisible?"). Tilted off your center, pulled out of your comfort zone in this strange new world, you must find a way to connect with others who might meet your needs. For safety's sake, you need to belong. Right now, you need to know where the bathroom is.

With the art of Negotiation two years ago, you could handle the simple barters of the social world of a four. Now, as a six, you find the needs and wants within and around you are wider and deeper, more intricate. No longer are you negotiating a win-win for two simple desires of two little people. Now there are glittering, hard-edged, complex needs and wants that would require six layers of wins on each side, if all were to be achieved. In this more complex environment—where you, yourself, have many needs and all the other kids do too—the ability to Compromise can be mined as the sixth **Childhood Treasure**, if you have the right tools at hand.

Mining the gem of Negotiation, at four, is about feeling your edges and the edges of those Negotiation boxes. It's waking up to the reality of the many edges on the many limit boxes around you. Four is about trying to find and line up comfortably with others' edges. Compromise, at six, is more about expanding yourself through connections to others.

In fact, this age of six is when you first have all the **Childhood Treasures** you need to begin the complex interpersonal interactions required in adult life. This is when that great three-part fuel starts to flow into your C.A.R.—Choice, Agency, and Responsibility are emerging now. You can begin to live your life and develop your relationships guided by your chosen values.

Compromise is clearly about choice. There is always a choice to be made in a compromise. What "want" am I willing to release to receive something else, which I want *more than* what I release? At its essence, Compromise is life's requirement that you make hard choices, choices that require you to release part of what you want to enable a greater good for yourself or a group. Maybe that group is just two individuals trying to get along in the sandbox of life; maybe it's a classroom full of peers.

Compromise is also agency: the art of choosing this action you value rather than that one. Agency is acting from your higher priority. At six short years of life, if the adults in your life helped you become someone who chooses her life, you had almost finished your early childhood mining job. If you received the tools and techniques you needed, you mined the Treasure of Compromise and life became defined by your conscious choices.

What is Acceptance?

Whenever compromises and choices are made, there is a need for Acceptance. When I choose, I must accept the consequences of my choice. When I compromise, I must accept the inherent loss in giving up part of what I want to get some of what I want. I must truly release, without regret, that which I choose to release. The only other choice is to carry the loss…forever. Release or hold on: those are your two choices. Then, Compromise also requires Acceptance of responsibility for the choice. I don't blame others for my decisions, my choices, my compromises, or my life.

See how the world suddenly got wider as you moved from your earliest years, at home or in child care or preschool, into the world of kindergarten and, now, first grade? That apparent expansion of the world continues through your seventh year, usually the final year of transitioning into a more logical approach to that world.

Now you reach the first steps to settling into early logic that is about the concrete world only. You can't yet be logical about abstract ideas, but for the first time, the world makes some real sense. It does not appear as random and magical as it seemed when you were three or four. As that logical sense emerges, in fact, it highlights the nonsense in the world; logic makes the illogical that much more visible. Your new understanding of cause and effect shines a spotlight's glare on those times when effect seems divorced from cause. This tension creates the perfect window of opportunity to mine the Treasure of Acceptance.

Here's what's going on. Sadly, you are beginning to notice that:
- Goodness, kindness, and innocence are sometimes rewarded with harm, cruelty, and manipulation. You're nice to someone and they're mean to you.
- Random acts of insanity or revenge can kill a plane full, a high-rise tower full, a restaurant full, or a classroom full of people.
- Sometimes people who love you do or say things that leave you feeling sad, angry, wounded, ashamed, or alone…and you don't know why.

You can't see a reasonable cause connected to these effects. People leave, people die; hurt and grief happen to perfectly nice people. And you can't do a single thing to prevent or stop that reality.

Here is where the adults in your life could have stepped up with some final tools to help you with your digging. To be mined, faceted from its rough state, and polished, the Treasure of Acceptance needs all the tools used to mine the first six Treasures plus a few more. In fact, the first six Treasures almost deliver an easy dig for number seven.

All that remains is to learn that life is not about you.

That's it. Acceptance is the certain realization that *only* the life happening inside your skin is about you. Sound familiar? Yes, the Treasure of Acceptance is the toddler's Treasure of Independence, grown up and with superpowers! With Acceptance, you can know absolutely that *nothing else* outside of your boundaries is very much, if at all, about you. Can you hear how liberating that is? Anything that is not your thought, your feeling, your interests, your body…is a mystery! If everything outside your skin is about someone else, life becomes continuous discovery! No more assuming that the gestures, tones of voice, facial expressions, and even verbal communications from others are instructions, criticisms, approvals, or other special messages for you to deduce and interpret.

With Acceptance fully mined and shining at the roof peak of your Little Red House, you get to wonder instead of interpret. Rather than assuming anger from someone who pokes and lightly hits you in the upper arm when she talks to you, you get to wonder: Does that woman poke and lightly hit everyone in the arm, or is it just me? In what kinds of circumstances does she do that? Is there any pattern to that behavior? I wonder why she does that. Acceptance shines when you achieve the perspective of an observer with genuine—I would even say *loving*—curiosity. Acceptance is a wide-open door, really, an invitation to bring a sense of wonder to the vast diversity of the world in which we live.

If you begin from the assumption that *everything anyone* else does represents what's going on inside *their* skin, you're operating from Acceptance. That sounds easy until the first time you find yourself saying that someone "made" you feel this way or that, or that you "had to" do this or that to prevent someone else feeling some way or other. Many of us speak as if we have no boundaries at all, even while professing autonomy of thought and feeling. Listen to yourself talk about your daily interactions with others. Do you assume you know what others think, feel, want, or need without ever asking them? If so, then it's time to get back to digging for Acceptance, or maybe even Independence!

Here's what may be a surprise: The "rest of life" that is not about you also includes your past. The ways your parents, siblings, friends, teachers, coworkers, and others hurt you, or even traumatized you, *was not about you*. You're not meant to spend the precious moments of the amazing gift that is your life in an endless recitation of past wounds. You don't have to invest the treasure of your adult life in managing the past. True release of the past's grip on the present is a sure sign that Acceptance has been mined.

That's what Acceptance is. It's freedom—true and utter freedom—to bring all of your grace-filled self to the true challenges of life. With Acceptance, we can be free from cringing or hiding away from, confronting and battling, or attempting to manage in some way all the feelings, interests, needs, and even thoughts of others. You get to let go of all that reacting to others' outward twitches that are manifesting their internal processes and get on with being your amazing Self-governed, Ego-aware, Leading, Free S.E.L.F., bringing your unique light into the pulsing light show that is life.

Maybe you found this capacity when you were seven years of age and rounding the corner from first grade into second. Maybe the raw ore still lies, quietly waiting, beneath a mighty pile of life's debris.

What if all seven of your **Childhood Treasures** lie there, in the dark, waiting?

Struggling Without the 7 Childhood Treasures?

The **Childhood Treasures** become smoothed and polished into anchor bolts for a "safe house." Remember? You venture out from this home base in your C.A.R.—your Choice-Agency-Responsibility mobile—into your relationships with others. If the home is shaky or the fuel supply insufficient, then adult relationships are continuously fraught with difficulty, drama, or trauma.

Beyond the specific examples on pp. 5-6, what is life like, generally, without these Treasures upholding the structure of your Little Red House? Let's look at the impact of this kind of life on the many relationships of family, work, and world that comprise a modern adult life.

For those who lack **Trust,** asking for help and accepting offers of help do not come easily. Without Trust, you might feel the need to rebuff praise or disbelieve compliments. Without Trust, you may struggle to delegate tasks you should or work cooperatively with a team. You may be unable to ask for just rewards for your work (e.g., praise or bonus). Those without Trust often struggle with the inability to form authentic and rich interpersonal bonds with others. Sadly, they may even question others' motives in wanting relationships with them. Even trusting that someone can care for them is too much trust.

When **Independence** is missing, you may take others' behavior and opinions personally, especially critical feedback about your performance, and become defensive. You might struggle to make decisions or stick with them; maybe you don't hold consistent beliefs or opinions and seem wishy-washy. Without Independence, we cannot live by our stated values because we are too susceptible to others' points of view. Instead of a rooted tree, we are just blowing leaves in the winds of interpersonal storms. Those without this Treasure may easily take on stories about others and treat them as fact, passing on undocumented gossip as if it was an observed reality. Those of us without Independence often do not know what we want or need. "I don't know" is the standard answer to any question about our internal life of feelings, desires, and opinions, as in, "Where do you want to go for lunch?" "I don't know. Where do you want to go?"

Without the Treasure of **Faith** in your life, you may lack passion or enthusiasm for the miracle of life. Maybe it is difficult to inspire you; you live in a sea of boredom, in awe of nothing. When Faith is missing, our negative attitude pervades work and relationships in a continuous stream of complaints. We live from the "life stinks and then you die" point of view. Maybe the lack of Faith shows in a lack of creativity, a sense of life as routine. Maybe you are just going through the motions of life and seem to be missing the point.

People without the Treasure of **Negotiation** have trouble getting along with others in small groups. If you lack Negotiation, you may be a pushover or doormat for those who are more assertive or aggressive, or you may be a bully who controls others. Those who cannot negotiate prefer to rely on rules or past patterns rather than responding to the situation in front of them. These are also the family members and coworkers who tattle on others, especially on those who bend the rules they hold sacred.

Without **Vision**, you may procrastinate or obsess over details. You may frequently feel as if your wheels are spinning and you're getting nowhere. If you struggle to form a goal, or have a goal but feel it is beyond you to design a plan to achieve it, then Vision needs more mining work. If you start projects but don't complete them (be honest—how many partially completed projects are in storage?), you likely need to polish up your Vision gem. Those of us who didn't mine our Vision completely at five years may be rule-bound and unable to think beyond the familiar. If you express a lot of negative thinking about the ability to get results (i.e., "We'll never get there!"), Vision may be missing from your Little Red House.

If you lack **Compromise,** you are likely stuck in "my-way-or-the-highway" thinking most of the time. You may have trouble finding middle ground when your point of view is starkly different from another's. As with a lack of Vision, you often lock yourself into an either/or approach between two obvious choices, missing all the variations that could be new opportunities. A lack of Compromise can also create somebody who subtly dismisses or overtly tears down alternate suggestions during a dialog or brainstorm. Maybe you hold onto your viewpoints rigidly, refusing to hear and consider other perspectives. Perhaps you have difficulty with diversity in a group or are uncomfortable with cultures and backgrounds different from your own.

Finally, when **Acceptance** is missing from your adult relationships, you are likely to hold tightly to past errors and hurts, still feeling the pain and still blaming the one who hurt you. You may be someone who resists change and fights against other nonnegotiables in life. Perhaps you feel you have little influence on life. Rather, you feel buffeted by life's

forces. Maybe you often say, "I had no choice," or blame your problems on a vague or unnamed "they" or "everybody."

This is life without the *7 Childhood Treasures*: afraid to trust those you care for; unable to express who you are, or maybe even uncertain of who that is; dispirited and bored with life. Is this you? Unable to get what you want, spinning your wheels and making little visible progress, afraid of the new and the possible, angry and hurting over the ancient past…?

That doesn't sound like a life anyone would choose if they knew there was another option.

Well, there is another option: life with a solidly built home for your Self-governed, Ego-aware, Leading, Free S.E.L.F., anchored in place with Trust, Independence, Faith, Negotiation, Vision, Compromise, and Acceptance, sparkling at every corner!

Got Treasures?

You can have a massive do-over of your early childhood years and start moving into your relationships powered by Choice, Agency, and Responsibility. Before you commit to the mining labor ahead, it's only fair to have at least a glimpse of what you're in for. So, what will life with the Treasures look like, in general?

**Trust.** When you are willing to depend on others and trust your needs will be met by them, who will you be? Most importantly, you will be a person who knows what she needs. You will be comfortable with the reality of needs and be 500 percent certain your needs are legitimate.

That term, "legitimate," seems to imply a required external judgment of validation, so that's not quite right. The certainty that comes with well-polished Trust is that your needs are a sort of birthright, for which you need neither apologize nor feel shame. I speak not of your myriad and ever-changing wants, mind you, but of your needs. For the essentials in life—like someone who sees you, hears you, and respects you—whom do you trust? For intimacy, shared passions in life, for validation and positive regard, on whom can you depend?

Those who have Trust also experience the peace and comfort of being cared for. To surrender temporarily to another, when we cannot care for ourselves, requires the vulnerability of trust. With Trust, we can choose to make ourselves that open and do so without fear. The reward is a deeply satisfying sense of safety and protection.

While none of us should ever live in a continuous state of feeling less powerful than a significant other, a beloved friend, or a close sibling, we can choose this vulnerability when appropriate. We can "delegate" some of our self-governance during physical illness, for example, or when recovering from injury or psychological trauma. At times of heightened emotions, such as extreme grief at the death of a beloved family member or friend, we can allow someone to be our good mother for a bit as we succumb to the wordless heartache of a younger self. During periods of intensive and exhausting personal growth or discovery, we can allow ourselves to be pampered and to rest while someone else stays in charge of life's basics for us.

With Trust in the foundation of our Little Red Houses, we have all these outcomes because we believe our needs can be met by others, and we allow ourselves to be vulnerable to their care. These are the two chief signals that the Treasure of Trust is integrated in our adult relationships.

 **Independence.** This Treasure co-anchors the foundation of your Little Red House. It allows you to discern what is you and yours from what is not. Seems simple enough, eh? Yet even the elegantly simple advice from Byron Katie to stay in your own business can be challenging.

The mining of Independence requires you to clearly define your business as your thoughts, your dreams, your emotions, and your body. Another's thoughts (especially *about* you), another's dreams, emotions, and body are not your business until that other person invites you into that business.

With the Treasure of Independence gleaming in your safe home's foundation, you find your point of view becomes just one story among many rather than the Truth for all. With this Treasure fully mined, we also come to truly understand that nobody else knows what we think, feel, or want unless we express it in a way they can witness and understand. We can enroll others in our thinking and dreaming only when we expressly share "our business" with them. That's right: even those who love you cannot be expected to read your mind or heart.

Living with Independence also brings a paradox. Yes, you sharply feel your human edges. You are aware of the physical skin that creates the edges of your body, along with the emotional, mental, and soul skins that create the edges of your feelings, thoughts, and dreams. You also become keenly aware of your *connections* to everyone else. Independence in your foundation means living 100 percent aware of your unique and separate self, and 100 percent aware of your complete immersion in groups: family, community, workplace, congregation, etc.

These two hallmarks of Independence—feeling our edges and knowing that we, as individuals, are part of myriad communities—allow us to take leadership in our own lives. With compassion and understanding for ourselves and others, and without isolation, we live separate and connected.

 **Faith.** What is the impact on your life when you become willing to believe in the impossible? Maybe that belief includes a deity, but—remember—the Treasure of Faith is not just about religious or spiritual beliefs. The impossible can be an impossible dream. When did you last dream a dream so big you could not see how one brief lifetime would be time enough to accomplish it? What if you still held that dream in your arms, gently tending and nurturing its life?

What is the impact of a Big Dream? What does it do to your life when you fervently pursue a goal so big you know you may not finish? Well, it expands you and your life. Wholehearted belief in and engagement with a worthy quest creates a larger life: a life full of joy and sense of purpose; a rewarding life; even a happy life. The same ups and downs, joys and sorrows, gifts and losses cycle through your life—that doesn't change. The quest makes *you* larger: in generosity, perspective, and the capacity to dream even more. You become more inclusive of diversity in your life and learn from experiences and dreams other than your own.

This deceptively simple little Treasure of the three-year-old child allows your mind, body, and spirit to soar beyond known limits. A well-polished Faith is the cornerstone of life for all creative geniuses, from Maya Angelou to William Faulkner, Marie Curie to Bill Gates, Mae West to Whoopi Goldberg, and from me to you. Faith allows you to believe in *yourself*, your own potential, as your life becomes the biggest dream of all.

Negotiation. This Treasure allows us to understand, see, and work consciously within the limits and agreements that shape relationships. We find ease in relationships through awareness that our emotional, intellectual, and energy "skins" are always finding ways to fit smoothly against the edges that others bring to this party we call life. Part skill, part art, Negotiation allows us to observe, somewhat dispassionately, the observable cues from friends, colleagues, and loved ones. These cues tell you where to find other people's edges so you can find your fit.

From patterns of verbal and nonverbal communication with your beloveds and acquaintances, you learn what they think, believe, want, dream, and feel. If you pay attention, you learn *their* ways of apprehending reality and their many *modus operandi* for navigating the complexities of adult life…and you don't judge. Negotiation works best when your observations are simply catalogued as what is observable about this person, without labeling it good or bad.

Accepting the reality of another's edges without judgment allows you to act in ways that acknowledge those edges, which makes relationships go pretty smoothly. With a partner whose physical boundary contains a couple of damaged knees, you'd be considered insensitive when suggesting a hike into and out of the Grand Canyon as a vacation. And when a colleague has hot-button reactivity to teasing, you are insensitive when you tease him. With a sibling who pursues a Big Dream to end hunger in America, you forward her links about others serving in the same way rather than encouraging her to pursue what *you* see as the more realistic and practical goal of cleaning out her basement.

Remember, Negotiation is about getting you what you want while also helping others get what they want. With this Treasure, we learn to make choices inside a box created by another person and to be clearer about our own boxes. Being able to negotiate for what you want, without denying others what they want, gives your relationships the sparkle of mutual respect and harmony. Rather than feeling a victim to others' more important goals or being a person whose goals always override the interests of others, you become an interpersonal collaborator. With Negotiation, your success with win-win relationships fosters your image as someone who "gets along with everyone."

**Vision**. With Vision in your life, you live with invention. You live a life that expresses your innate creativity. Yes, we all come wired for creativity! You may sing, play an instrument, act on stage, write prose or poetry, dance, paint, sculpt, or pursue some other activity you think of as art: weaving, beadwork, knitting, or crocheting. Or you may do something *artfully* you haven't, up to now, thought of as art: engaging in a sport, gardening, building from wood or stone, rearing or teaching children, or walking the difficult dogs at the shelter. This list is short compared to the wide sea of possibilities. For some, creativity is simply expressed as a general playfulness, a sort of pixie/fairy approach to daily life as if it's a fun game to be played.

Viewing the world from a creative, inventive point of view, you see and reach for what is outside the usual box. You get BIG ideas. Impractical ideas may come slamming into your heart. From the practical facet of this Treasure, you are also someone who easily and confidently sets goals, makes plans to achieve the goals, and brings those plans to fruition—even for those impractical ideas! With Vision integrated into your Little Red House and life, you decide to get a task done and it gets done. Procrastination is for others, not you! Jump up! Dive in! Just do it!

Only a few of us survived kindergarten and first grade with this sense of efficacy and creativity intact. So, if your Little Red House contains this beautifully shining asset now, then you are often seen by others as the creative one and/or the one who gets things done. A life with Vision means you can be a leader in most groups you join.

**Compromise**. One of the most cherished attributes in any workplace, service team, or family is the ability to compromise. When you live with this Treasure gleaming in the home of your being, you are not just *willing* but are fundamentally oriented toward finding resolution.

It's second nature for you to look, not for differences, but for common ground and shared understanding. You listen to hear others' goals, needs, and interests and ask for clarification if you're not sure. You spontaneously offer solutions that already include the interests of others. You take other people into account in your plans and *don't sacrifice your own interests* to theirs. Ahhh! There's the rub. A lot of you readers were nodding along, thinking you have this Treasure nailed until we got to that part.

Compromise is never about giving up who you are or what you want—at least not all of it. When you dance artfully with this Treasure, sorting and sifting priorities, you always satisfy some of your own goals, needs, and interests right along with those of your friends, colleagues, and loved ones.

Those who are most accomplished at Compromise are those who are clear about the values that guide their lives. Think about it. When you have five goals and need to release one or two as part of a compromise, what could be more helpful than a solid set of values to guide the elimination process? For example, if you value both, is it more important to be factual or to be kind? To have the best argument in a debate or to foster authentic connection with a loved one?

Choosing any course of action already implies a letting go of all the other possible options. Compromise, especially when it is value-driven, enables confident and peaceful release of that which must be released for the sake of that which is chosen.

Compromise in the roof of my Little Red House is also revealed by how I find the intersections of who I am with the wide, wide world of diversity around me. Notice, please, that I did not say how I "cope with" diversity or "deal with," or even respect or embrace. When I hold diversity as something separate from me, something about which I *do* something, I am denying that diversity is the essence of the world's condition. Diversity is something of which I am a part—in so many ways, indeed, in every way. With Compromise, I simply accept that I am *one* of billions upon billions of creative expressions on this planet and in the universe, and I play joyfully with *every other one* I encounter.

**Acceptance.** Living in oneness with life's diversity, I no longer see myself as being passively affected or victimized by it. Neither do I feel any need to control it. I experience myself as an agent in my own life. I recognize the great gift of choice and rest peacefully in the certain knowledge that I choose the condition of my life. If circumstances anywhere are beyond my endurance, I can make a change to those circumstances by changing my thinking about them, or I can go somewhere else, do something else.

At its essence, this Treasure is "living in the now," as Eckhart Tolle extols; it is "loving what is," as Byron Katie advises. Because in *reality*—in that flow of activity that happens around and within us—sometimes "bad things" appear to occur. The now, or "what is," sometimes shows up for us as a negative, a harm, or just an annoyance. With Acceptance as the roof cap on my home of self, I respond to such appearances with a shrug of my mental shoulders. As a fascinated observer of life, I can notice the apparent negative with interest, as the mystery it is.

There it is: I've described a life lived with the *7 Childhood Treasures* as one in which we:
- Believe our needs can be met by others.
- Allow ourselves to be vulnerable to others.
- Take leadership in our own lives.
- Have compassion and understanding for ourselves and others.
- Are connected, rather than isolated.
- Believe in ourselves.
- Are diplomats, successful with win-win solutions.
- Live a life of invention, a life that expresses our innate creativity.
- Joyfully find intersections between our unique selves and others within a world of diversity.
- Feel ourselves as agents in our own lives.

If this list does not describe your life, and you'd like it to, then read on! Let's get mining!

Good News! It's Never Too Late to Mine!

Whether you are reading this book at twenty-six, forty-six, or sixty-six, it is never too late to return to this early childhood work of mining for the *7 Childhood Treasures*. Why? As long as you're living, you are in relationships that matter to you, and you can improve those relationships with this work.

That's not a baseless boast, either. Most of those who have taken my workshops, classes, and intensives since 2005 have told me how deeply this framework has changed their lives. In some rare cases, I have had the honor and pleasure of watching the mining work of a friend or colleague, seeing the day-to-day digging, prying, faceting, and polishing. I have witnessed the birth of boundaries—of Independence—in a woman of fifty-five. I saw the first awareness that healthy Trust is possible sparking in a participant's eyes as we completed the *Trust Who for What?* Exercise (pp. 57-63).

Whether you seek in your relationships a greater sense of mutual respect and support, more honesty and authenticity, deeper intimacy, or expanded spontaneity; whether you hope for less drama, release of worry, receding strife; or just plain clear communication…if you find and polish up your Treasures, you are sure to improve things. Never mind the other person. You're the only person you can change. Just get digging for your own birthright, and the rest will follow.

That's what the rest of this book is about. To the child you once were, you can be a parent now. You can do over the developmental processes of those first seven years. The activities ahead will let you be the parent you needed then, but in a way that works for you now as an adult. The Development Do-Over tools are not for children but mirror the pathway young children walk.

You may find yourself stumbling upon an additional lode of work that needs some deeper digging, perhaps with a spiritual advisor or therapist. For some of us, a return to the early years is to remember and relive trauma, toxic stress, and other adverse experiences. Licensed clinicians and spiritual practitioners are an important resource for that part of the work.

Always remember that the Treasures are still there, waiting for you to come and rescue them from under the slag heap of your life's experiences. If you didn't mine them then, you can mine them now and build your Little Red House for a Self-governed, Ego-aware, Leading, Free S.E.L.F.

It's never too late to begin. So, let's do that!

A Final Reminder

As we get down to mining the Treasures, let's remember *why* you are willing to do this work. Trust, Independence, Faith, Negotiation, Vision, Compromise, and Acceptance do each have their own value. Plus, unearthing the Treasures gives you the anchor bolts for a strong safe house, secure from the storms of life. As you build your Little Red House, you become a Self-governed, Ego-aware, Leading, and Free person—your S.E.L.F.! Yet we can't stay home forever.

The greater purpose for building this home is enabling your S.E.L.F. to generate the fuels of Choice, Agency, and Responsibility—for the C.A.R. to carry you into your relationships. Living as your S.E.L.F., you have plenty of fuel to power your engine!

Self-governed. Self-governance, or personal sovereignty, means having *authority* over your own life. It means being the intentional author of your story in the world. That is, self-governing women and men are those with the agency (initiative or power) to freely express their unique perspective, gifts, and quirks in the world, in ways that do not harm others and often add value to others' lives. They are the authors, the creators, of their lives rather than the responders to a life created by others for them. Self-governance includes owning the responsibility for their impact on others when they deny or damage another's sense of value, even unintentionally.

Ego-aware means knowing how your human mind works, for example, how your brain works continuously at high speed to create stories that may not be fully true. To become aware of the ego and its many strategies for distracting and deceiving you is to enhance your ability to act by choice, to live on purpose, moving from intentions rather than acting out your pain. Ego-awareness also guides you in taking responsibility for your wake in life, showing you your accountability for wounds—however unintentional—to others.

Leading. Remember, living as a S.E.L.F. means responsibly governing *your* life and staying the heck out of any efforts to govern anyone else's life. Your self-governance holds the reins to your life lightly and does not snatch the reins of others' lives and pull them along with you. Acting as a leader in your own life simply means that you go first, with your own agency. You make the first play, as in a card game. Those who lead their lives don't wait to be told what to do next…and they often have many followers. These kinds of leaders are followed more compared to those who seek to drag folks into compliance or to control them.

Free. The first freedom that comes with mining the *7 Childhood Treasures* is a simple and obvious one. You will become free from your own self-imposed limits. You will stop holding yourself back from life with fearful rules restricting your choices. You also will free yourself from long-believed falsehoods about who you are, which were imposed on you before you understood the dynamics of ego. I can't guarantee your body never will be incarcerated or restrained against your will. I can promise that, with the Treasures in your Little Red House, you will be free in your own mind, regardless of any chains, bars, or locks limiting your body.

So, just to be clear, having committed to return to your own mining work, unfinished in your early years, you are not committing anyone else. Your family and close friends have not agreed to share this task with you or to commit to their own *7 Treasures* mining. Don't confuse your personal intention for a group project!

As you engage in the self-discovery and internal changes that will result from this work, please be aware that they will transform you. That's a given. Your relationships will need to adjust to how you are changing, and that will become a series of negotiations with others who have value, just as you do, regardless of where they are in life's journey.

Alrighty, then. Ready? Put on your helmet and turn on the headlamp. Sling a pickaxe over your shoulder. Here we go!

Find Your Trust

To find the seam of the rough ore of Trust, buried deeply beneath all the years since your first year, we begin by looking at how trust lives in your relationships now. One simple mental model for trust and one deceptively simple exercise that generates profound results will let you see how and where you trust now.

First, the simple mental model: What if you had an internal Trust-o-Meter to measure how much you trust in any given situation or with any given person? It could be similar to a thermometer, with a red liquid that rises and falls to indicate low or high trust on a scale of zero (no trust) to 100 (completely trusting).

How does your Trust-o-Meter respond to new opportunities to let others meet your needs? When you enter a new group or meet a new person, how high does your Trust rise and how quickly? Do you start at zero, with an "earn my trust" approach? Or do you start at 100 percent and let your trust fall away as others betray your trust? Jot some notes about your patterns here:

_____
_____
_____
_____

Next, how is your start-up trust affected by group characteristics? If someone has a different color skin or a different religion from yours, is your beginning trust less compared to someone of your own skin color or religion? Do you trust men differently than women upon first meeting? If someone looks poor or out-of-style in their clothing, does that affect your first level of trust? What about if someone has a certain kind of accent? or has a bumper sticker for a particular political party? or whose body is very heavy or extremely thin? What external features of a newly met person tell you that you can trust or not trust him or her? Jot your thoughts:

Finally, what behaviors in others lead to an increase or decrease in your trust? Does a broken promise or an unmet expectation plummet your meter from 100 percent to zero percent all at once? Does zero percent rocket to 100 percent when you receive a little pat on the head, a touch of approval? When someone agrees with your politics or admires your work? Does your trust rise in small, measured increments, each hard-won by your new friend's evidence of trustworthiness, yet always remain on the verge of plummeting to zero again at a misunderstanding? Make some notes here about these behaviors:

_____

_____

_____

Facing these questions fearlessly and answering them honestly is the first step in finding and extracting the raw ore of Trust still buried within you. Release your fear of your own or others' judgments about *how* you trust and just notice how it works for you right now. All of us come to adulthood with stereotypes that affect our trust of others; it's human. Let yourself discover how you trust in new situations, how you respond to the outer trappings of a new person or group. Just notice for a while: observing yourself and your trust responses.

Many of us have the pattern of a zero percent or 100 percent initial trust. We either trust nobody at all or trust everyone completely. These two responses arise from our fundamental beliefs about people. Either we believe people are out for themselves, insensitive, and lacking in compassion, or we believe people are essentially good, loving, and connected to us. Interestingly, those who tend to believe in the goodness of others and trust *everyone* fully from the start often also have a hidden mistrust. Hiding behind that abundance of trust is the expectation that it will be betrayed. In this case, the Trust-o-Meter's measure of complete trust drops like a stone to the lowest level over a misunderstanding. In truth, both of these default settings of the Trust-o-Meter are equally unhelpful in our relationships as adults.

The Trust-o-Meter is a good mental model from which to begin, but its simplicity doesn't tell the whole story. Actually, trust is not this simple. Once you understand the basic dynamics of trust using this simple up/down model, then it's time to get more sophisticated.

The truth about Trust is that it's not an all-or-nothing proposition. We talk about trust as if it is just that, as in, "I don't trust him/her." Though there may be some people with whom we have no trust at all, it's not as common as you might think. The truth is, if someone is in your life in a significant way, then you either trust them for *something* or, I'd hope, it's a court-ordered relationship. Why else would you let someone in your life that you cannot trust for anything you need?

The question that helps us mine the **Childhood Treasure** of Trust, the *adult* question to ask about Trust, is "Whom do I trust for what?" Not "who do I trust/not trust," but "whom for what?" To answer this question, you must first know what you need from people with whom you have relationships.

Yes. *Need*. Just hearing the word evokes a range of emotions in people—from nervous to excruciatingly fearful. Remember, the infant learns trust by having her physical and social needs met, through repeated experiences of the pattern *I need, someone comes, need met*. How much you trust, whom you trust, and for what requires you to understand your needs. So, what are they? What are your needs?

Trust Whom for What?

This exercise is not about what you *want* in life, like a new car or a bigger closet. This is about your *relationship needs* as a person. What do you need from other people? What are your emotional, spiritual, intellectual, and physical needs that are fulfilled—or you *wish* were fulfilled—through your relationships with others? Record them below or in the center column of a piece of paper divided into three columns, like so:

	My Needs	

In the grid below, I've listed a few of my needs in relationships; I have many more. Notice that I included a mix of physical, emotional, intellectual, and spiritual needs in my list. Take some time now to start your three-column chart like this and list your own needs. Before you read on to the next step in the exercise, it's best to pause and do this step.

	My Needs	
	Physical closeness without sex	
	Positive regard; glad to see me	
	Praise for accomplishment	
	Sounding board for raw, uncut emotions	
	Equal exchange of ideas	
	Laughter and playfulness	
	Connecting in metaphysical and physical Oneness	
	Shared quality time together	

Here's some guidance on needs ….

Perhaps you cannot think of anything you need. This is a sure sign you need to mine the Treasure of Trust. Can you trust me enough to try this exercise? Can you trust me when I tell you that each of us does have needs, even if they are deeply hidden from our own awareness?

In a crosswalk of key needs identified by psychologists Roy Baumeister, William Glasser, and Abraham Maslow, I have found this core set of hot-button needs we all share. When we're not getting these needs met, we feel friendless, unloved, and alone:

- A unique identity that is *seen* by those we love ("I need to be seen for who I am.")
- Certainty of our worth, a sense of self-esteem ("I need my value to be recognized.")
- Power, a belief in our agency and the significance of our impact ("I need my power honored.")
- Belonging, being loved, connection, relationship, community ("I need to be loved.")

If you're struggling to identify needs you have, then you can safely start by assuming you have some versions of these four. Try to describe what the behavior of a loved one *looks like* when they are meeting these needs for you. For example, you might list as a need related to the second point, as I did, "Positive regard; glad to see me."

Whether you've listed one or many needs, I suggest you sit with your list and let it grow for a week or three. Keep adding rows as you think of, or experience, more needs you have. Notice your needs. Notice those moments in daily interactions with loved ones and coworkers when someone disappoints you with their behavior. Likely, they just failed to meet a need you have. What was it?

In the times when you feel betrayed or let down, ask yourself, "What need did I have that didn't get met?" We adults are cagey about needing things from each other; our needs tend to play below our conscious awareness. Encourage them up out of the subconscious shadows into the light, out of the shame we feel about having them, and into the radiance of ownership.

Yes, we have needs. All of us have needs. We're *supposed* to have them. They're part of our birthright!

Did you learn you're not supposed to have needs? That having needs makes you needy, and that it's too unattractive or too vulnerable to be that? Perhaps you might consider these facts:

- Of all the species, humans have the longest childhood dependence on adult caretaking. That dependence keeps getting longer for some, with "children" living at home to age twenty-six and beyond!
- We have, throughout our history as a species, been tribal; we've lived in extended families or communities as an intricate, interdependent web of mutual support and commerce.
- In all the major and in most of the lesser-known religious traditions, surrendering oneself into the care of an omnipotent, omnipresent, and all-knowing divine force is the highest expression of faith.

It seems clear to me that we are programmed to need each other, no matter how unpleasant that may sound to you. Even if you find yourself resistant to finding and stating your needs, see whether you can let your resistance soften a little. The ability to find and mine the raw ore of Trust begins with the ability to name the needs you have. Once you know them, you can learn to trust their fulfillment to others.

Now that you're aware of some of your interpersonal needs and you've "sat with them," reflecting on them for a little while, it's time to move on to step two. Let's look at who meets the needs you have.

In the left column of your original chart, which is on p. 58, write the name of at least one person who meets that need 85 to 90 percent of the time. (Those who meet your needs are allowed to not be perfect; they get an off day every now and then, just as you do.)

Here are mine, with names changed to protect my innocent friends and family members:

Who Meets My Needs (85-90%)	My Needs	
Women friends (many); spiritual community (lots of huggers)	Physical closeness without sex	
Jane,* Mellia, Gillian, Sandy, Mandy, Ronald, more…	Positive regard; glad to see me	
Alice, Marla, Gillian, Mandy	Praise for accomplishment	
Alice, Sandy, Gillian, Shania, Mellia, Candace	Sounding board for raw emotion	
Alice, Sandy, Candace, Mellia, Gillian, Shania	Equal exchange of ideas	
Candace, Sandy, Gillian, Jane, myself	Laughter and playfulness	
Sandy, Mellia, Mandy, Gillian, myself	Connecting in metaphysical Oneness	
Mellia, Gillian, Shania	Shared quality time together	
*All names changed to protect my loved ones and me!		

Notice that naming yourself as someone who meets one or more of your needs is perfectly acceptable. Take a few moments to fill out the left side of your three-column grid on p. 58 (or on your separate page), adding names of individuals you can trust to meet each of your individual needs. Remember, you're not looking for individuals who meet *every* need on your list. Need by need, who is there for *that* need?

Certainly, you will name some individuals more than once. You might even find that you name the same person as meeting many, or most, of your needs. It's important to look at that pattern, and others, such as:

- *You* are meeting all or most of your needs.
- You can't think of anyone in your life who meets any of your listed needs, including yourself.
- Your primary life partner/spouse is *not* listed as meeting *any* of your needs.

What are you learning about how your capacity for trust is working? Is there more trust in more of your relationships than you previously thought, or less?

Next, we're going to look at a third aspect of trusting others to meet our interpersonal needs. Who *does not* meet these needs—ever, or at least less than 5 percent of the time? (Even those who don't typically meet your needs may offer a flash of supportiveness once in a while.) For each need, name one or more individuals who have proven unable to meet that need on repeated occasions. Here's my list:

Who Meets My Needs (85-90%)	My Needs	Cannot Meet My Needs (>5%)
Women friends (many); spiritual community (lots of huggers)	Physical closeness without sex	Ronnie, Kirlin
Jane, Mellia, Gillian, Sandy, Mandy, Ronald, more....	Positive regard; glad to see me	Ronnie
Alice, Marcia, Gillian, Mandy	Praise for accomplishment	Jane
Alice, Sandy, Gillian, Shania, Mellia, Candace	Sounding board for raw emotion	Jane
Alice, Sandy, Candace, Mellia, Gillian, Shania	Equal exchange of ideas	Ronnie, Kirlin
Candace, Sandy, Gillian, Jane, myself	Laughter and playfulness	Creighton
Sandy, Mellia, Mandy, Gillian	Connecting in metaphysical Oneness	Jane
Mellia, Gillian, Shania	Shared quality time together	Lorna

Take some time now to complete your grid's third column.

Here's where analysis of your patterns can get really interesting! Take a look at each need, who you said meets that need, and who cannot. Now, just focused on one need, circle the name of the person in that row to whom you most often turn to *try* to get that need met. As I once did, do you have a pattern of trying to get that need met by someone who can't meet it? Meanwhile, are you ignoring a person who is ready and willing to meet that need?

Are you turning, over and over, to a dry well to slake your thirst when there is a steady flow of water within reach?

What if the person who is most important to you right now is not meeting any of, or very few of, your needs? What do you want to do about that? Certainly, opting out of that relationship is one path, but it's not usually necessary for this reason alone. Most people who love us are willing to learn to meet our needs if we can be clear about what we need and help them learn what fulfills that need for us. Often, all we have to do is ask. By the time you finish this whole book, you could be ready. Maybe you're ready now.

Now that you understand some of the complexities of Trust in your relationships, you can return to the simpler Trust-o-Meter as a helpful tool. If you want to become more attuned to your needs and help those who love you to meet those needs, then incremental change is the place to begin. Rather than assuming either a zero percent or 100 percent trust in anyone, notice *how much* you trust each person and for which specific needs.

Here's what I mean: I can trust my dear friend Alice as a sounding board for any raw, unprocessed emotional reaction I may have to anyone or any event in my life. Whether I'm afraid, angry, or wildly confused, Alice listens to my rant of words that grope for the meaning of my experience. She doesn't judge, try to fix me, or tell me about her problem that is "just the same," only worse. She tells me I am smart and loving and perfect. She asks gently probing questions that lead me to my own discovery about what to do. Alice is highly trustworthy in this response, based on my many years of experience.

What if I see that Alice is likely to also be someone with whom I could connect in metaphysical Oneness? Rather than transferring my 90 percent trust for Alice's role as a sounding board to this new area of need all at once, I take it slowly. Based on years of Alice sometimes sharing her spiritual experiences and feelings, I might express a modest level of my need at a time when I'm not feeling urgent or desperate. Maybe I ask her to sit and breathe together with me for a short meditation at a time when I'm feeling slightly stressed. If that goes well—which, for me, means that Alice joins me in this experience and expresses enjoyment in it—then I may one day call her when I'm really in need of connection and ask her to join me in prayer or take some other small next step.

The point is that I take small steps toward 90 percent trust, allowing the Trust-o-Meter to rise slowly in response to my actual experience of trustworthiness *with a particular need*. Even if I come to 90 percent trust of Alice to meet this new—to her—area of my need, I still don't automatically assume that level of trust for other needs.

You see, the Trust-o-Meter's simple up and down metric is meant to work that way—neither always at 100 percent or zero percent nor leaping from zero to the top. Neither should it plummet from 100 percent to zero after one event. This measure is meant to move up and down by small degrees, in response to an *actual experience* with someone.

Too often, our trust responses to others have nothing to do with their actual behavior or ability to meet our needs. Instead, we trust people who look like us, speak like us, remind us of our parent or sibling relationships from childhood, or match some fantasy story we hold about what a trustworthy person is like. Such blind trust is part of what psychology refers to as confirmation bias, which is common in humans. It explains why neighbors of mass killers are often surprised. Their "quiet" and "nice enough" neighbor, who "kept to himself," was trusted for the wrong reasons.

Living as a Self-governed, Ego-aware, Leading, Free S.E.L.F., it is part of your job description to do this work of finding out how you trust now, then beginning to extract, mine, and polish the ***Childhood Treasure*** of Trust by:

- Getting honest about the fact that you have interpersonal needs
- Allowing others to meet at least some of your interpersonal needs
- Becoming clear about who can meet which of your needs…and who cannot.
- Asking others to fulfill your needs in low-stakes ways before asking them to fulfill a big, hairy, audacious Need
- Helping loved ones learn what your needs are and how to meet them
- Letting loved ones teach you the same about their needs
- Noticing when you're setting up yourself—and someone else—for failure by asking her to meet a need she is constitutionally incapable of meeting.
- Ending the patterns of going to a dry well—bringing one of your needs, over and over, to a person who cannot meet it

Excavate Your Independence

Now, you've started the digging at the very bottom, at your first year of life. Each layer of mining will become a little easier as you move back up through the archaeological strata of your life. Each new Treasure you mine benefits from the mining that has gone before, and this is especially true of Trust and Independence! They are the foundations, the concrete footings, of your Little Red House.

To offer you a look at your Treasure of Independence, I use the simple checklist that follows and a mental model based on the phases of the moon. Each of these two tools shares a perspective—one intellectual and one more emotional—on how you hold your own in relationships. Then, I offer you the challenge of beginning to question your own version of reality.

Let me clearly say that the checklist that follows is in no way a valid or reliable psychometric assessment or evaluation. I do not propose that it be used to diagnose any psychological or behavioral health category. It's a simple checklist to give you a general idea about the health of your boundaries of body, mind, soul, and emotion. These boundaries are the essence of the Treasure of Independence (see pp. 25-28 for a reminder about boundaries).

Don't think too long about any one item on the checklist. Just ask yourself: Is this statement very true, kind of true, or not true about me? Go with the first answer that comes to you. You can be as honest as you dare, as you're the only one who will ever see your answers and final score.

We'll use the checklist as a tool to inform your understanding of how boundaries manifest and how you've done in creating and hanging onto your own set of "skins."

Boundaries Checklist

		Very True	Kind of True	Not True
1	I feel that I have no self of my own.	0	5	10
2	I sometimes adopt the values, thoughts, feelings, or desires of someone else when I don't know what mine are.	0	5	10
3	I often ignore my body's needs or best interests.	0	5	10
4	I sometimes let my needs take a back seat to the needs of another.	5	10	15
5	I mostly can't hold my own and just give in to what others want.	5	10	15
6	I push my body's needs to one side because they inconvenience me or someone else.	5	10	15
7	Rather than have a different opinion or need, I often agree with what others believe or think (or I stay silent).	5	10	15
8	Simply and clearly—without aggression or defensiveness—I can express what I believe, what I feel, and what I want.	5	10	15
9	I can, without aggression or defensiveness, listen to others express what they believe, feel, and want.	10	5	0
10	I know what my body wants and needs for food, exercise, and rest, and can supply it or ask for it.	15	10	5
11	I can calmly state my own interests without feeling the need to qualify or explain them.	15	10	5
12	I compromise who I am to avoid being different or to avoid disagreement or confrontation.	5	10	15
13	I have recently said to someone close to me, "Here's what I think, feel, want…," while feeling that I am perfectly okay—no guilt, no worry.	15	10	5
14	I have recently disagreed with someone else's ideas or had feelings different from another's and known I was acceptable in my difference, and so was the other person—both of us perfectly okay and different.	10	5	0
15	I am willing to consider another point of view, desire, or feeling other than my own—really consider it as a possibility for myself—without needing to aggressively defend myself.	15	10	5
16	What I know is what I know. I don't listen to others' opinions.	0	5	10
17	I make sure I get what I need and want, even at the inconvenience of others. They should stick up for themselves.	0	5	10
18	I don't talk about myself much; my secrets are mine to keep.	5	10	15

		Very True	Kind of True	Not True
19	I often overshare, telling people too much about myself too soon.	5	10	15
20	My needs and interests are so strong that there is no room for others'.	0	5	10
21	I am confident that my thoughts/feelings/desires are the best or most important—the only ones worth having.	5	10	15
22	I hug or touch others without first getting their consent.	5	10	15
23	I often tell somebody my life story within the first hour I know him/her.	5	10	15
24	I physically dominate others with aggression or threats of aggression.	0	10	15
25	I often find myself explaining, in depth, why I have a certain belief, value, or feeling, either trying to convert someone else to it or at least validate it in her/his eyes.	5	10	15
	Total Each Column:	___	___	___

Add the 3 column totals together _____ + _____ + _____ = _____ **GRAND TOTAL**

(See p. 130 for the scoring key)

Moon Boundaries

Now that you know the status of your boundaries from this intellectual perspective, let's look at a more emotional perspective. The phases of the moon make beautiful metaphors for boundaries.

For this mental model, I invite you to abandon scientific knowledge and pretend the moon generates its own light. If you can't pretend, then perhaps you can find a cellular memory. Can you find that little bit of DNA that remembers how the twenty-five-times great-grandparents of the twenty-five-times great-grandparents of your twenty-five-times great-grandparents saw the moon?

Two millennia ago, your ancestors didn't know the moon is a large rock reflecting the light of the sun. They didn't know that the moon *seems* to shrink, go dark, and then regrow because of its orbit around the earth. All they knew was that the moon shone full and became dark in a cycle of phases that told of the passing seasons on their land. That moon had its own light, as far as they knew, and it had a lot, a little, or none at all.

So, I invite you to pretend or remember this *other* reality: The moon glows with its own light. In a person, that light stands for her or his unique thoughts, feelings, and desires or longings. Imagine these stages of waxing and waning light as images for your Treasure of Independence—some healthy, some compromised. You may want to read the following descriptions of those images with a journal or paper and pen at hand, reflecting on and recording your answers to any of the questions that strike you as relevant.

Dark moon, new moon. This moon sheds no light at all. If you are far enough from civilization's artificial lights, you can see its outline—a slightly lighter gray circle around a dark gray disk against an even darker sky—so you know it's there. It's as if the moon's light has been replaced by something else. Its light has been eaten up, covered over. Its body seems to have disappeared into another body. Moon could not keep out what was not-moon, and so its unique light has been replaced by an "other."

"Whatever you want is fine, dear." Sound familiar? Have you ever been the dark moon, with boundaries so permeable that you simply "became" someone else—adopted what they thought, felt, needed, and desired? Have you ever felt you had no self of your own, that maybe even your body did not belong to you? When have you acted as if your body didn't exist or didn't deserve your attention? Have your boundaries ever let your desires, beliefs, or body's needs be completely eclipsed, grayed out, overshadowed by the self or needs of someone else? Jot your thoughts here:

_____

_____

_____

_____

New crescent or balsamic (waning) crescent. These two moons shine with very little light; only a sliver of self is contained by the boundaries of these moons. Like the dark moon, their boundaries could not entirely keep out what was not them, and so their unique lights have been compromised, pushed to one side by those of another or several others.

Do the new and balsamic crescents provide an image of your boundaries? Have you ever felt that little of your thoughts, feelings, desires, and values could hold their own against those of your friends, partners, coworkers, or family members? Do you hear judgment of your worth in their comments and questions about your life, especially from traditional authority figures like Mom and Dad? Have you ever pushed your body's needs to one side because they would inconvenience you or someone else? When have you found yourself willing to give in to what others believed or thought rather than express a different opinion or need? Have you ever compromised who you are to avoid being different, prevent conflict or disagreement, keep the peace, or keep from rocking the boat? Make some notes:

Gibbous (waxing) and disseminating (waning) moons. I see these three-quarter moons as the images of healthy boundaries. This is the Treasure of Independence in the image of the moon. Almost fully rounded, but with clear and distinct edges, these moons shine with enough light to be seen for the full disks they really are. Yet their edges are flexible enough to interact with the darkness around them. These moon phases are independent but not isolated. They take in new ideas and consider them. They are empathetic to the feelings of others. They can get excited with someone about a new adventure that is not their adventure. Someone with gibbous/disseminating boundaries lives life on her or his own terms and never feels inferior to someone else who has chosen different terms.

Are your boundaries like the gibbous and disseminating moons? Do you not only know who you are, but can you—simply, clearly, without aggression or defensiveness—express what you believe, feel, and want? Can you, without judgment of self or others, listen to others express what they believe, feel, and want, simply accepting the differences between them and you? Can you say, "Here's what I think, feel, want…," while feeling you are perfectly okay, that you are not "too" something: perhaps needy, bossy, or demanding? Can you consider another point of view without needing to aggressively defend your own viewpoint? Record your thoughts here:

Full moon. This moon's light shines beyond its boundary. Its boundary is overpermeable in the opposite direction from the new moon. The full moon overshines; its light radiates past its edges, out onto/into the night sky around it. Its body invades the space around it rather than interacting with it, as do the three-quarter moons.

Are your boundaries like those of the full moon? Do you ever shine your light so brightly that there is no room for the lights of others? Are you confident that your thoughts/feelings/desires are the most important, the only ones worth having, the capital-T Truth? Have you ever found yourself oversharing, telling people too much about yourself too soon? Do you tell some people your life story within the first hour you know them? Do you press your beliefs or values on others, trying to convert them? How are you the full moon?

_____

_____

_____

As you read these questions and answer them, you may find that your boundaries are not always the same. Maybe in some situations or with some individuals, you allow your selfhood to be subsumed by theirs, while you overshine/overshare with others, and have healthy boundaries with a third set. Once you know what you do, then you can begin to decide whether it works for you as a S.E.L.F.

If you feel resentment, fear, or even mild concern about the lack of self-governing, ego-aware, leading, and free choices your S.E.L.F. is making in any relationship, then strengthening your boundaries is your first work. And it is *your* work. How fully you bring your light to a relationship is not about anyone else or what they do. It's all on you…and *knowing* that—with 100 percent conviction—is a good sign that Independence is mined.

Question Reality

The key to polishing Independence to its gleaming glory—the key to having healthy boundaries—is the realization that "reality" is simply a story we tell ourselves. In our already-always-talking monkey mind (a.k.a. the neocortex of the brain), sensory input is a supersized fire hose of incoming data about actual reality from which we each take only tiny, uniquely selected sips. We mostly lap up only those droplets of reality that fit well with our already formed stories.

Think of yourself as a land of a million lakes, with each lake a story you've formed using selected drops of reality. We each keep our lakes contained and add to them, as we can, with our sips from the hose. Then, sometimes, a river of reality—new data—rushes in, bursting the dam and flooding the land. In these moments, the calm surface of our sense of reality splashes open. Whole past realities may drain away, almost in an instant. Maybe several other pools of reality re-form, creating a new set of lakes.

It's easy to think of childhood examples of these overhauls to the story landscape. Think of the first time you knew there was no Santa Claus or Tooth Fairy or other magical being in whom you had fervently believed for years. Think of the first time you realized that a sturdy adult was completely at sea, flying by the seat of his pants, or completely lost. That first moment of seeing a competent adult's vulnerability, when you know *they don't know*, can be a shock.

There is solid science behind this fanciful and watery imagery for our stories. From the intersection of physics and biology, we know that human sensory organs cannot possibly perceive all of reality. Matter is not really solid but is constantly moving energy and lots of open space. There are likely dimensions beyond the four we perceive, including time. So, your first filter on the incoming super flood of data is your own limited perceptual abilities. Then, about half of what enters is quickly filtered out as your mind classifies it as irrelevant. These sights, sounds, and sensations are so commonplace, you no longer perceive them for long spaces of time: sounds from our always-turned-on, high-powered world; scents from our own bodies; a breeze across the skin…

The half-load of data still flowing at this point hits another layer of filters to create meaning. The neocortex looks for sips from the hose that perfectly fit into existing lakes. Each pond of story pulls in the data that are most meaningful to that already written story. Oh, *that* works, and *that*. Oh, good, here's more fitting what I already know to be true. This isn't just you; it's everybody! The human mind is designed to see when data fit well and can be assimilated into what is already understood.

For a moment, think about this from the point of view of a young meaning-maker. A toddler learning to name things in the world often learns "dog" as the first name for a four-legged, furry being. So, when she first sees a cat, goat, or yak, it also lands in the reality lake named "dog." Eventually, enough additional data, often in the form of corrections ("No, sweetie, that's not a dog, that's a cat."), lead to formation of a large network of small ponds, each for a species and all connected into the larger body of water called "animals." This network of puddles, ponds, pools, and lakes become the child's categorization of the animal kingdom.

All this explanation is to say that the first tool for mining Independence is to **Question Reality**. Yes, a motto similar to the moral, "Question Authority," from the fable "The Emperor's New Clothes" is what you need. In this case, you question *your* authority to determine reality.

Questioning Reality begins with accepting you can't possibly know what really happened between you and your friend or child or partner because your series of filters took all the edges off, handling it with the hands of your past experience, looking for meaning. Now, what you "remember" happening is really a story of meaning you've created. You pieced together a few bytes of information with the glue of your existing view of the world. For building healthier boundaries, I highly recommend you always begin by *constantly* questioning your certainty about…well, everything you think you "know!" Those who know Byron Katie's "The Work" will remember that the first question to ask is "Is it true?" and the second question is "Can you absolutely know that it's true?" Questioning Reality means you will soon be admitting that you cannot *absolutely* know much at all!

The hard truth is that your memory of the interaction with a loved one is not a video that faithfully records reality. In fact, there is simply no such thing as one capital-R Reality that we all share. Your memory, your codified story of meaning, is based on your experience, is unique to you, and is formed by this known process.

First, there is the continuous flow of activity all around you. Stuff happens. People talk, walk, kiss, yell, steal, love, hit, die, and need you. Life comes at us every day at 1,000 miles per second, offering a complex, rich, multilayered tapestry of sensory data to interpret. That's the **Real Reality**, out there in the physical world outside our skin. We can measure the light waves, sound waves, and shock waves entering our bodies every nanosecond of every day. But *none of us* really knows that reality *at all* because those waves of data come washing into a set of foundational filters unique to every individual.

Then, the sensory data we absorb hit a multi-funnel sorting system that lines up with all our fundamental understandings of the world in which we live. One of us has a funnel called "Dangerous World," while another has a funnel named "Safe World." Another has a funnel called "You Get What You Fight For," while a fourth has a funnel called "No Matter What, Be Kind."

You have maybe ten or twenty of these *positional perspectives* on the world—broad beliefs so fundamental to who you are, you are not fully aware of them (unless you've spent some serious time exploring and analyzing yourself). You mostly formed these fundamental or core beliefs about how the world operates and who people are before you could fully understand the world or could effectively communicate in it. This wholly internal and **Personal Reality** is comprised of the fairy tales of your childhood, codified in a set of basic commandments about life. Here are some more possibilities:

- People are naturally good and kind.
- Everybody is out for his own self-interest; nobody really cares about anybody else.
- Life's a sh*t sandwich, and every day you take another bite.
- Life is an unfolding, rich miracle where anything is possible.
- Families take care of one another.
- I'm safe when I have control.
- I only get what I'm smart and brave enough to take.
- People will do what I want if they're scared of me.
- Love can heal anything.

Here's the thing about your Personal Reality: It's a powerful set of filters! If incoming data can't sort themselves into one of less than two dozen funnels of your reality, typically, they are simply lost. You disregard them as irrelevant. Real Reality comes in through your sensory organs, and you immediately lose about 80 percent of it because these Personal Reality filters don't recognize it. Period.

Then comes the next set of filters, smaller funnels that are about specific groups of people: men or women, as a gender; rich people or poor people, as a class; black and brown people or white people, as a skin color; fat people or skinny people, as a body size. This **Ism Reality** is a second layer of your personal reality. Rather than tell you how all people are or how all of life operates, these internal realities tell you how subgroups are and behave. For example:

- Men only want one thing.
- Women are overly emotional.
- Black and brown people are less intelligent than white people.
- White people are all slave masters at heart.
- Fat people are lazy.
- Rich people are heartless.

By now, you've further whittled down the amount of Real Reality you're working with as you strive to understand what's happening around you. You've got about 10 percent of the data from Real Reality left to aid your understanding.

The final filter is your history of personal experience, nicely summed up by an old-fashioned word rarely used anymore: your ken. Your ken is your sum of knowledge and understanding; it is the final defining of your perception that leads to your **Story of Reality**. This is the stage at which your emotions join the story. Your personal experiential history, including all your emotional reactions to that history—your ken—lends meaning to what you've created from your Personal Reality and your Isms. The Story Reality is not the Real Reality that occurred out there beyond your skin before your sensory organs began receiving it, any more than a sketch of an apple is the fruit itself. What is left over at this point is a shadow of that original reality, a little sliver of it left after all your filters have shaved off its "meaningless" features. That filtered reality created an emotional echo in your history to make meaning that is personal to you.

The flood of data from Real Reality is the same for each of us, before we individually apprehend it with our sensory organs, and then—in a segment of time too short to name—each of us has made it into a unique Story Reality by sending it through these various sorters, sifters, and shapers. We have interpreted the data from within our meaning framework…and think we know what occurred. But ten individuals in the same experience have ten different stories to tell.

Two-column journaling. This tool has proven helpful in separating, as much as I can, my Personal Reality from Real Reality to see the latter more clearly. Take some time after an upsetting interaction with someone to write about what happened in this format. Divide your page into two columns, and first, on the right side, record your Story Reality of what happened. Then on the left side, record the most accurate, objective version you can of the actual words and behavior as they occurred. It might look something like this:

What Actually Happened	What it Meant to Me
His voice sounded loud and his brow furrowed.	He was so angry and mean!
He mentioned my recent weight gain.	He really went for my jugular.
I got choked up and cried; I couldn't speak.	I don't know when I've been more hurt.

If you separate each statement of your Personal Reality's feelings/reactions, you will find it easier to think back and locate the observable, objective cue from Real Reality (e.g., facial expression, tone of voice, body language, words) that links to the meaning you made of it.

I do also recommend Byron Katie's "The Work." I found her approach and tools extremely powerful yet easy to understand and simple to use. Essentially, it's four questions you ask yourself about any particular Story Reality you might hold. You can watch videos of her engaging people in this process on her website.

So, **Question Reality** is the lead tool for strengthening your boundaries. Stop assuming what you understood to happen *is* what happened. Stop thinking that your Story Reality is The Truth. Start by asking yourself, anytime you feel hurt or angry, "What if my feelings aren't about what really happened?" or "Am I sure I know what really happened?" Ask yourself, "What if there's another story/explanation here?" or, simply, "What if what I think is true is not true?"

Gather Your Faith

You can expect to keep digging for the first two treasures of Trust and Independence. The simple checklists, mental models, and reflective exercises I offered were just a beginning. Remember, no longer are you merely cutting through the original, careful crust, laid down to protect the Treasures until it was time for them to emerge in your childhood. Now you're excavating through decades of life's slag heap.

You know about slag, right? Also called "cinder," slag is the more or less fused matter remaining from the extraction of a metal from its ore. Slag vitrifies, or turns to glass, as it cools, similarly to how lava hardens into obsidian.

All the false starts in your early childhood mining efforts—those times when the Treasure was ready but the tools you were handed were insufficient to the task—generated some of this slag in a new layer that buried those developmental ores within. The process you're engaged in now requires busting through some tough strata. How tough depends on the volume of drama and trauma in your first seven years of life. Keep chipping away, my friend, for as long as it takes because the end result has more value than you might imagine now.

To know whether Faith is holding up one wall of your Little Red House, simply look at the indicators embedded in your life. Faith isn't about whether you go to church, temple, or mosque, or whether you keep the laws, commandments, and traditions of your faith. The **Childhood Treasure** of Faith is broader. It's your overall awe for, and engagement with, life's miracle.

As a gentle reflection on your current level of Faith, I invite you to pause for a little while from your reading and do a bit of continuous Journaling. This practice involves writing in response to a prompt statement or question for a specified period of time without stopping.

If you can't think of anything to say, then write that down. Whatever comes into your mind—"This is stupid. I can't believe I'm trying this. This is too woo-woo for me. I can never think of what to write when I journal…."—WHATEVER comes to your mind, just write it down and keep on writing. Go back to the prompt statements now and then, as in: "She wants me to write about my experience of passion, and I don't know what to say. I…"

Be the Dory (from *Finding Nemo*) of journaling: "Just keep writing. Just keep writing…" Eventually, your mind may calm down from its distracting chat with itself and allow you to write something meaningful to yourself. If the first effort doesn't yield much meaning, try again. Try a few times before you dismiss the value of this tool. It can generate amazing results.

So, journaling novices should begin by setting a timer for fifteen minutes—just long enough to break through that monkey-mind chatter, but not so long that it feels like forever—or thirty minutes if you're accustomed to journaling or adventurous in your personal growth. Write and write and write about any of these three prompts or any combination of them:
- An experience of the world that took your breath away or brought tears to your eyes
- A time you felt deeply humbled and grateful to be alive
- Your passion for changing the world in a specific way (e.g., ending human trafficking, creating more green space, rescuing and neutering feral cats)

Ready? Got your favorite paper and writing tools? Have you turned off your phone and minimized any other likely distractions? Got the timer ready? Okay! Ready! Start the timer…and write!

I hope you did take a break to do that journaling and that it gives you something to look at now. Did you find a way to talk about all of these experiences? Two or one of them? If you didn't, what did you find yourself writing instead?

Did what you wrote indicate that you are often inspired in your life? Do you have a life mission that your own enthusiasm drives you toward? Can you feel the simple and overwhelming miracle that is the universe as we know it?

Or does most of what you wrote reveal a lack of direction, lack of passion, or lack of energy for the larger experience of life beyond earning and consuming; beyond working, paying bills, and saving for retirement; beyond doing what's expected and safe?

While you wash dishes or vacuum, analyze spreadsheets or make follow-up calls to contacts, change the diaper or fix dinner, are you aware there is more to life? Do you know why you choose to do *these* activities as your mundane routines in life? Are you present as you do them? What else do these mundane tasks enable? Why are you here if not just to tick off items on a daily task list? What is your life meant to do besides perpetuate its own routines? For what are you willing to give your life? For what are you living?

These are the questions Faith asks us to answer. This is the **Childhood Treasure** that first comes to the surface when we shift our toddler-vision focus out to the wider world. Faith is the Treasure of discovery. As young children, we lifted our gazes from a few years of inward focus (*my*

Trust for you, *my* Independence and boundaries that identify *who I am*), and suddenly we became aware there was some pretty interesting stuff going on *around* us as well as within us.

If a genuine, heartfelt sense of life's many miracles eludes you, then it is time to start your mining of Faith. To find the Big Dream of your life, it is helpful to begin by dreaming. Here is a short two-part exercise to take you into that dream.

Someone Could

For part one, take a few minutes to make a list in response to this prompt: "Someone could…" and end that statement with some changes you believe would improve the world. Maybe someone could create more of something or less of something. Maybe someone could create something brand new or put an end to something entirely? Maybe someone could reduce or eliminate child hunger, animal abuse, elder abuse, or pollution of our watersheds. Maybe someone could plant more trees, create more public art, or hold politicians more accountable.

Make a list of everything you would like to see someone do to change the world. Go ahead! Fall asleep to the world in which such things are impossible, are too big to tackle, and dream instead of the perfect world. Yours might include changes as simple as George Carlin's wonderful dream of an "idiot gun" to shoot suction cup darts with flags that say "IDIOT" onto the cars of bad drivers. Here's a place to make your list, or feel free to use a separate page or your journal:

_____

_____

_____

_____

_____

_____

_____

Now that you have your list, I invite you to read it aloud to yourself. Yes, the whole list. Out loud. Go ahead: Start each one with "Someone could…" and read them all aloud. "Someone could…"

Do any of them seem to pull at your heart more than the others? Do some make you sit up a little straighter or cause a catch of emotion in your voice? Do any bring a tear to your eye? Whichever ones those are, mark them in some way. Then, I invite you to read those marked items again, changing the beginning of each statement to "We could…"

Set aside for a moment any feelings of fear or resistance you may be having to stating that you "could" be a part of doing these things. These statements are just tools to measure your responses… so notice those responses. Notice the fear, maybe panic, at the idea of tackling some big change in the world. Notice the voice in your head that tells you that the dream is beyond your abilities, impossible to achieve, or crazy. Say, "Thank you for that perspective; I'll keep that in mind as I explore."

Now, say the statements that have the biggest impact on you again, this time beginning "I could…" Can you find the one statement that seems to pluck your heartstrings when you begin "I could…"—the one that vibrates you the most? Then repeat that one aloud in this way: stand up, place your feet in a solid stance with balance and grounded strength, take two or three big breaths deep into your belly, and exhale them slowly. After the next big breath, say "I could…" and that statement.

How does that feel? Do you find a resonating energy inside that says YES to this idea that you could change this important aspect of our world? Do you feel terrified and full of self-doubt at the same time? That's probably a Big Dream for you to pursue.

If you feel you have found a Big Dream that could capture your interest for a lifetime, then you're ready for part two. If not, you may want to wait a few days and try part one again. If Faith was truly quashed in your third year of life, as it is for many children, then this kind of dream process may need a few repeats to shake you loose from your disbelief in your power to change the world.

If, as part of your early childhood experience, your imagination was also flattened, then the guided imagery exercise that is part two may not work well for you. If you have a hard time imagining pictures or scenery, you may want to move past this activity to the one that follows it.

When you're ready for this visualization exercise, you may want to consider beginning by recording the guiding language below, which you can then play back, letting your own voice guide you through the images. Read slowly, saying each word clearly and distinctly, and using a timepiece that shows the passage of seconds to guide you in leaving gaps of eight to ten seconds at each pause [P] in the description. If your pacing is right, your recording should be about 10 minutes long.

Big Dream Journey. Allow yourself to relax and let go of the world around you, the world just before *you* begin at your skin. [P] Focus on your breath coming in and going out, and allow that to relax you. [P] As you continue to breathe, you find your mind focuses inward, letting go of the movement and sound around you. [P] You may close your eyes or leave them open but unfocused on any object in the world as you keep breathing and relaxing. [P]

Imagine a big spiral laid out on the ground before you. [P] See its color and form, clearly visible against a background. [P] Notice you are standing at the outermost tail of the spiral where it ends its final coil, several circles out from the center point of the spiral. [P] Imagine that this is you, today, facing a spiraling path into the future. [P] Notice the sweep of the concentric circles, starting at your feet and coiling into the center. [P] See the width of the spaces between the coils and the length of the spiraling line that is your path forward. [P]

Blink your eyes or flutter your eyelids a bit to shift your perspective. Now you are standing at the center point of the spiral looking outward. [P] From here, you can see that outer-circle tail where you stood moments ago and all the coiling, concentric circles to the center where you now stand. [P] Imagine that this spiral is part of your life's timeline and you are at the end point of achieving your Big Dream. [P] The change you want to see in the world has come to pass and you are there to see it. [P] See yourself stand at this moment in your life when you know your Big Dream has come true. [P] Feel the emotions that are part of this significant moment. [P] Look around you and see who else is there to celebrate the momentous occasion. [P] Notice the posture of your body and the energy that fills it. [P] What is it like to be at this point of "mission accomplished"? [P]

Now, imagine you can turn around and look one step back from this end point upon which you stand. [P] One step behind you on that last coil is the last step that brought you to this end point. [P] What do you imagine as the last step you took before the Dream was realized? [P] What changed or what occurred in the world as the final step to fulfilling this Big Dream? [P] Can you also imagine the last change before that one? [P] Look a little farther back along the spiral's path to the preceding step before the last one. [P] What can you see that must have happened or changed a bit earlier to achieve this mission? [P] Can you see one more step before that one too? [P]

Once again, blink your eyes or flutter your eyelids a bit to shift yourself to the outer tail of the spiral. [P] Back here in the present time, looking down at the path into the future, [P] what is the first step before you? [P] Can you see, in the first few inches of that line, a step that would lead you toward the final changes you saw when you looked back from the future? [P] What is that first step? [P] What change will happen first? [P] And can you see one more step down the spiral beyond that first step? [P] What might be the second change you pursue to get to that glorious ending point? [P]

Now, let your mental focus leave the spiral of a Big Dream both fulfilled and begun. [P] Bring your mind's eye back to this place and this time. [P] Hear the sounds of this moment happening all around you. [P] When you're ready, allow your eyelids to open and focus on what is before you.

I recommend you jot down a few notes about the imagery your mind created in response to this guidance so you remember it later. Use the space here or use a separate page or your journal.

(lined writing space)

Now you might have a sense of how a Big Dream can fill your life and become the real reason you get out of bed every morning.

Be the White Queen

If visualizing and other imagination activities feel uncomfortable or "don't work" for you, we may need to pump up your muscles of imagination, your ability to invent. To quote one of my favorite singer-songwriters, Holly Near, "Can you call on your imagination, as if telling a myth to a child? Put in the fantastical, wonderful, magical; add the romantic, the brave, and the wild!" Let's pretend together, like we did when we were children. In this case, we will imagine ourselves to be the White Queen from Lewis Carroll's *Through the Looking-Glass*.

We all remember the Red Queen offing everyone's heads, but do you remember the White Queen in Wonderland? Alice laughingly tells the White Queen, "There's no use trying…one can't believe impossible things." The Queen replies, "I daresay you haven't had much practice… When I was your age, I always did it for half-an-hour a day. Why, sometimes I've believed as many as six impossible things before breakfast."

So, let's *first* pretend to be the White Queen! Imagine what you might be like if you were this character. Here is an original illustration to help you get started, but don't let it limit you. And don't let a picture be your only image. Hear your regal voice and feel your stride as you walk, knowing you are the White Queen! Feel the energy of your power as you pass your subjects, waving. Can you catch a whiff of your own royal air upon the breeze?

What is the White Queen like *as you*? A modern day, twenty-first-century White Queen may not be like what the original nineteenth-century illustrator, John Tenniel, thought. Other reinterpretations of the White Queen since the late 1800s also may not capture her quite the way you see your internal White Queen. Look at this image for a little inspiration to your imagination— maybe even look online for some more options, like Anne Hathaway's movie role version.

Breathe in and out slowly as you look at each image, following your breath with your mind, even as your mind processes the data from your eyes. In-spire. Breathe in and let your inspiration light your imagination, like a breath of wind fuels a spark into flame.

Now, close your eyes and experience your internal White Queen, using all your senses. Answer some or all of these questions about her, as you gaze with your inward-seeing eyes and hear with internal ears:

- What gender is your White monarch: Is she a queen or a king? Both? Neither?
- How tall is your White Queen, and with what body build?
- Notice your White Queen's hair color and style, eye color and shape.
- What clothing has your White Queen chosen for a costume?
- How does your body move as the White Queen?
- What is the weight of your regal robes?
- How does your royal cologne smell?

Jot some notes about your image of the White Queen in you or, if you're so inclined, draw a sketch:

_____
_____
_____
_____
_____
_____
_____
_____

Now that you have met your White Queen, let's put her to work imagining impossible things! What is on your list of "not possible"? It's crucial to know all the possibilities upon which you shut a door of low expectations. What do you tell yourself is not possible? As in, "I'll never be able to…" If you can identify those dreams you've labeled as unattainable, then you can deliver the antidote to such a lack of Faith: imagining these "impossible" dreams coming to fruition.

I invite you to use the grid below or a separate page you divide into two columns, with these words at the top of the left side: *I'll never be able to…* Now, let your mind and pen wander while you capture all the endings to that sentence popping into your mind. *I'll never be able to reach my goal weight. I'll never be able to sing at Carnegie Hall. I'll never be able to find a soul mate for the rest of my life.* "I'll never be able to…" What's your list?

I'll never be able to…	

Now comes the White Queen bit. Below, or at the top of the right side of your page, write: *My Big Dream is to…* Below that, beside each of your "impossibilities," let the White Queen in you write the affirmative, present-tense, honest version of this event as a reality. Call her up, as you did moments ago in response to the questions about her. Then let her tell you the impossible affirmative opposite for each item. For example, *I'll never be able to reach my goal weight* becomes *I'm alive and thrive at 155! I'll never be able to sing at Carnegie Hall* transforms to *My singing takes me wherever I seek to go.* A statement like *I'll never be able to find a soul mate for the rest of my life* becomes *I am blessed with loving support and soul-deep connections for the rest of my life.*

I'll never be able to…	My Big Dream is to…

Yes, these affirmative statements, when truthful, are less prescriptive than your anti-Faith messages. That is the nature of Faith and Big Dreams, as well as the nature of physics, but that's another book for another day. Essentially, overprescribing the details of a Big Dream's outcome is like trying to predict exactly what you'll look like in thirty years. You may achieve what you prescribe in the details, or you may come close but end up saying, "Well, that was unexpected!"

Meanwhile, your list of perceived limitations morphs into your list of "impossible" things to imagine—as the White Queen advises, "as many as six before breakfast" every day! Consider six a *beginning* dose of Faith prescribed by Dr. Scott. You're going to gradually build up to a therapeutic dose of imagining. To take your first dose, simply read aloud one or more of your affirmative statements each morning. Read one six times over or read six different ones, whichever you like.

After three consecutive days of this dosage, add fifteen seconds of "Be the Dream" time after each statement. If you're speaking one statement six times, say all six then add the feeling time. To Be the Dream, simply close your eyes and sit with the statement for at least fifteen seconds. Hear, feel, and/or see what it is like for that statement to be true for you. Then move on to the next one if you're speaking more than one. (By the way, fifteen seconds is longer than you think; I suggest setting a timer.)

After three consecutive days of this dosage, narrow your list of statements down. Pick just one or two to repeat. If just one, repeat it aloud six times and then spend thirty seconds of Be the Dream time. If two, repeat one of them six times, add thirty seconds of experiencing it, then repeat these steps with the second Big Dream.

Continue at this dosage for three more days. The final increase in dosage adds outward expression. Whatever sensory experiences you have been having of one of your dreams, *express* them.

If it's a visual experience for you, draw or paint it, write a description of it, or describe it aloud into a recording device or to a trusted loved one. If it's an auditory experience for you, capture it in a melody or song lyrics, or choreograph dance or other movement that expresses what you hear. Perhaps the Dream has been mostly felt kinesthetically in your body. Express it with movement or postures, acting it out wordlessly as a mime would do.

Let your own way of sensing the Dream and your own deep wisdom guide you in your expression. The important piece of this experience is to *express*—let your internal experience out into the world and capture it in some way that is lasting…even if only in memory.

There you go, mate. That's imagination!

Exercising your imagination, identifying Big Dreams and seeing them as possible, giving yourself and your life into their keeping—these are the tools to use when mining the **Childhood Treasure** of Faith. The more you open yourself to "the art of the possible," the more you will find yourself awestruck by life's wonders and *vice versa*! The more you allow yourself to see the everyday miracles in the world around you, the more you will open your reach toward the stars, to dreaming your impossible dreams.

Mine Your Negotiation

Collectively, these first three **Childhood Treasures** enable huge doses of honesty, closeness, and joy in most adult relationships. Remember, Trust and Independence are the foundation of your Little Red House, and Faith is the top of one wall, raised above Trust. Next, you add the art of Negotiation, raised above Independence to form the second wall. This four-square reality provides a little shelter for your S.E.L.F. As you continue to refine your gems of Trust, Independence, and Faith, the remaining Treasures will be easier to mine and install in your safe home base.

Do you remember the developmental hallmark of the four-year-old (pp. 30-33)? Your wide-open, three-year-old arms were suddenly crossed over your little rib cage. The "I BELIEVE!" stance of the three-year-old shifted to a feet-planted Missouri mule saying, "Show me." This is the age when it's all about the rules, the law, being fair, and being right. When you meet an adult who is hung up on rules and fairness, or the chronic need to defend her "rightness," you are interacting with someone who is still stuck in this mine shaft to Negotiation.

This is the age at which we start to *really* figure out how to live in a world of other people. Up until four, the world had been all about you…including being smitten by the wonder of the wider world, mostly for the way it thrilled *you* (again).

At four, we finally began to really focus our attention on other people. This is the age at which you started caring whether you got invited to the birthday party, and "You can't come to my party!" became the worst punishment another child could hurl at you.

Yes, four years of age is when the thrill of narcissistic chaos *should* begin to give way to logic. At four, we start to figure out this fact of life: A group of egocentric dreamers can't get much done without some other tools. It's the perfect time to start noticing others' points of view, different from our own. We become curious about what makes people tick. We begin to understand that group efforts require shared purpose across differences.

When you were four, you wanted to know the *why* behind every rule you must follow and every limit on your exploration. This is the age at which children should be admitted to law school because, at four, we were very, *very* good at building our case and arguing a point. If children are supported in this budding set of basic skills for living and working in teams and partnership, they grow up to be good at identifying what they want and trying to get it for themselves, yet in a way that also respects what others want.

But what if disagreeing with adults wasn't permitted in your household or your child care? What if your early, rough-around-the-edges efforts at negotiating for what you wanted were seen as noncompliant, willful, disrespectful, or "uppity" in some way? What if you were punished, and your efforts to understand how others' interests can fit with your own were blocked and shunned as *wrong* rather than seen as an age-appropriate and temporary stage of your development? Well, then, let's get to work mining that capacity now!

The best way to assess the soundness of this new junction in your Little Red House is to look at your parents' parenting style. Many of us cannot accurately remember our parents' strategies of decades ago, though. Two proxies for this memory are: 1) your parents' current behavior, if they're still living, toward young children (or their own aging parents), and 2) *your* own behavior toward children. You are the echo of your parents' parenting style, brought into the present. Without conscious and conscientious effort to change, if needed, we all simply treat children as we were treated as children.

Below are some cues and clues about the mining status for your Treasure of Negotiation. Mark which ones sound most like one of the following: 1) your memory of how your parents parented you, 2) your observations of how they grandparent or otherwise interact with children or dependent seniors now, or 3) how *you* tend to parent/grandparent or interact with children.

Inhibit Capacity for Negotiation	Foster Capacity for Negotiation
Required to share toys before ~3 years of age	Encouraged to make decisions reasonable for age, such as clothing and food options
Required to wear clothes you didn't like; allowed no choices in your clothing	Given the option to refuse some activities, especially those that primarily affected you
Required to eat food you didn't want; allowed no choices in what to eat	Emotions validated as real, and expression of them encouraged
Told "don't cry/yell or be so loud" (don't be sad, don't be mad, don't be joyful)	Expressions of wants and desires encouraged
Cajoled, tricked, or persuaded into wanting what the adult wanted, not what you wanted	Wants and desires taken into consideration; fulfilled whenever reasonable

Inhibit Capacity for Negotiation	Foster Capacity for Negotiation
Mocked for or "talked out of" your ideas or beliefs that were different, unique	Expression of unique ideas and beliefs encouraged, met with interest
Punished for having ideas or beliefs that were different, unique	Encouraged and enabled to see all the many choices embedded in daily life
Told you had "no choice" but to obey parental commands	Encouraged to question and explore; invited to initiate and innovate
Told "do what I say and don't ask questions" or "do what I say, not what I do"	Afforded privacy, and personal possessions respected
Denied privacy or personal possessions	Asked about feelings/emotions
Told how to feel, e.g., "you should be ashamed," or "there's no reason to cry," or "you should be grateful/happy," or "you can't hate," or "don't act ugly"	Self-determination about physical contact with other adults supported and enforced, if needed
Required to let people hug or kiss you when you were reluctant, timid, or fearful	Boundaries of physical body protected from violent or sexually inappropriate touch
Any form of hitting (spanking, slapping, pinching, or more severe physical abuse), especially before age 6	Valued, loved, and embraced for the fullness of your unique self
Any form of contact with your "private parts" that was not for hygiene or health care	Given information to help you understand events that affected you
Punished for telling adults "no" or refusing their requests/demands in other ways	
Mocked, rejected, punished, or excluded for expressing your unique talents	How many in each column were true for your parents or for you?
Your dreams and desires were laughed at or labeled "impossible"	

It can be difficult to face these realities in our parents' (or our own) behavior. None of us means to limit children. We're just doing what we know to do, what we learned from the generational transmission of parenting lore in our families. Do you see? You don't have to be abused to come out of childhood with some baggage. Most parents really don't know how to support the development of emotional health and intelligence. Let's assume you've got some baggage or you wouldn't still be reading this book.

So…ready to continue unpacking that baggage? Let's start with the boxes.

Negotiation Boxes

From the time you were very little, you *might* have been learning about the Negotiation Boxes created by other people in our world. More typically, most people live in such boxes utterly unaware of them. When you were four, yours were built mostly by the adults in your life, if they had mined their respective Treasure of Negotiation. Negotiation Boxes are formed by **limits** that are consciously established for you (e.g., no jumping on the couch) and **agreements** forged with you (e.g., can we agree you'll have one more story before bed?) or affirmed for you (e.g., we shake hands when meeting new people) by adults.

Limits and Agreements make up the sides of every Negotiation Box.

Limits and Agreements. When you were a preschooler, you probably had little or no say in the limits or how they were enforced. Likewise, you may have held no role in the making of agreements with adults in your life or how *they* upheld them. Perhaps, instead of consistent limits and agreements, you grew up mystified about ever-changing "rules."

Maybe a behavior sometimes led to punishment and other times to reward, or to no response at all. Maybe adults' agreements with you were consistently maintained and honorably fulfilled. Maybe parents and teachers only randomly complied with these agreements or completely disregarded or denied them: "I never agreed to that!"

Whether consistently or mysteriously enforced, limits and agreements formed little boxes into which you were placed, day in and day out. These boxes may have been strong, with firm and stable sides, or maybe they were shaky, with sagging or trembling walls. Ideally, from inside some of these boxes, you may have developed the skills to discern their sides. Within those boxes, you also learned that you had room to move, to negotiate. You began to see that "rules" (limits and agreements) are not always simple, binary choices of on/off, yes/no, good/bad. Rather, they are ranges—defined spans of finite possibility. Again, I emphasize, this is the way it is *supposed* to work; it may not have unfolded this way in your childhood, which is why my description may sound confusing.

But let's step back a minute for some defining and clarifying. What are limits and agreements, exactly? The easy answer is they are the "no" and "yes" elements of any situation. A no (limit) tells you something you cannot (or, more likely, *should* not) do; a yes (agreement) tells you something that is acceptable to do or expected of you.

Agreements come from several sources: 1) cultural, 2) interpersonal, and 3) intrapersonal. These are, respectively, 1) agreements fostered by social groups, 2) agreements crafted between two individuals or in small and intensely connected groups, and 3) those crafted with ourselves.

Here are some examples of all three:

AGREEMENTS		
Cultural	Interpersonal	Intrapersonal
Women should keep their bodies covered modestly, including their hair.	As a young married couple, we decide that neither of us will get a tattoo unless we both do it.	I will do an hour of yoga daily.
Spitting in public is impolite, especially in mixed company.	As a group of siblings, we agree that we will not fight our parents' estate plans.	I will laugh along with jokes about my receding hairline.
Children should be seen and not heard.	As the two parents of our children, we agree that we will not hit them for punishment.	I will indulge in only two squares of dark chocolate a day!
It's rude to stop by someone else's home without an invitation.	As a senior couple married for more than fifty years, we agree to be open to new love after one of us is deceased.	When I have $15,000 in savings, I will start looking for a house to buy.

You may have noticed that some of these cultural agreement examples are gender- or age-specific or are from a different time or culture than the one in which you live now. You also may notice most of these agreements are broad in scope, but agreements also can be quite narrow in what they define. Not surprisingly, limits can also be categorized in this way.

Let's look at some parts of a sample Negotiation Box designed for a preschooler's lunch. Mom's opening question, in what *should* be a negotiation with her four-year-old son, is, "Would you like grilled cheese with tomato soup or PB&J with sliced apples?" Some of the invisible agreements implicit in Mom's Negotiation Box for her son are:

- Lunch can only include ingredients we have in the house already. (Intrapersonal)
- Meals must be healthy and nutritionally balanced across the day. (Cultural)
- We're going out tonight for Mexican food. (Interpersonal, with Dad)

Her son, learning to discern what agreements and limits form the walls of his choices, takes a stab at his opening position in the negotiation, striving to stay within this Negotiation Box. He counters, "Could I have cheese cubes, peanut butter, sliced apples, and crackers…and eat a picnic on the porch?"

Notice how cleverly he pulls ingredients from Mom's menu and reconfigures them into a different lunch that also fits into Mom's agreements! Cheese from the grilled cheese sandwich, peanut butter from the PB&J, and an assumption of the crackers that most certainly would have come with the tomato soup—the kid's a budding peace negotiator!

How do limits work with agreements to complete the sides of a Negotiation Box? Remember, each limit is a no. Let's say Mom says no to: 1) all added sugar in her son's diet, 2) taking her Mexican pottery soup bowls outside, and 3) complex menus for lunch. It looks like our young secretary of state has again stayed inside Mom's Negotiation Box with his alternative. A smart mom, a mom intentionally rearing children with all their **Childhood Treasures**, will say yes to this kind of inside-the-box alternative every time. She even will praise her son for his excellent negotiation skills!

Remember, the child in the above example is *you*, so now let's bring this dynamic into an adult example. How are you placed into Negotiation Boxes in your daily life now? Let's look at a possible box related to your work life.

Let's say your supervisor has made known these explicit expectations, or "yes" items in the sides of her Negotiation Box:

- Lots of face time in the office
- Regular updates on project implementation
- Immediately informing her when you can see that you will be more than forty-eight hours beyond a deadline for any component of a project

These expectations become shared agreements with you by virtue of your choice to keep the job rather than quitting. Probably, your supervisor also has some limits she has spelled out for you. Maybe her "no" list includes:

- Don't bring me a problem without talking about solutions.
- No whining/no excuses.
- No blaming others.

Already understanding these "yes" and "no" sides of your Negotiation Box, you get an email from her saying she's heard from a member of your team that your current project is headed for the ditch. You think you know who has tattled, and it's the team member who is actually the one holding up the timeline. Inside the box of your supervisor's limits and agreements, you could:

- Get a face-to-face meeting as quickly as possible and let her know that the project has a minor delay, off-track by less than thirty-six hours, and you are on top of supporting the team member who is currently moving the project forward. Clearly state your responsibility for getting things back on track.
- Ask the probable tattler to join you and one other team member for a short presentation to your supervisor on the project status. Ask them to prep with you, and then do a dry run of the presentation together before seeing the boss.

These two strategies probably fit inside your boss's Negotiation Box for you. What else might fit? What can you see that surely would NOT fit?

Can you see how a four-year-old child might make a sort of game out of this process with a willing adult? Although a child this age is developmentally programmed to negotiate, his first efforts are likely to be clumsy and miss the target of the box. Going back to our lunch choice example, an early attempt to negotiate might go like this: Parent offers lunch options of PB&J or tomato soup with crackers, and child counters with a request for tacos.

If Mom is willing to patiently help him learn the sides of her Negotiation Box, then the child can get better and better and better at negotiating inside it. In this case, Mom might calmly reply, "We don't have any taco shells right now, so tacos are not an option. Plus, Daddy and I already decided we're all going out for Mexican tonight, so you can get your tacos for dinner! For lunch, we have everything I need for you to have a PB&J or some tomato soup with crackers. Which one of those would you like?" Mom also could help the child mine the Treasure of Negotiation by sharing the information that the next trip to the grocery store on Saturday will be when we can get some taco shells in the cupboard.

Younger miners for Negotiation (~forty- to forty-four-month-olds) might give up at this point. Mom will know that the Treasure of Negotiation has begun to surface when the child keeps going. If the next statement from the child is something like, "Well, do we have cheese?" This question shows that the child has grasped the concept of an established limit or agreement. In this case, the agreement the child is learning is "We have to have it in the house."

Today's Negotiation Boxes for You. Mining Negotiation as an adult requires us to become aware of the Negotiation Boxes we're in and also those we build for others. The latter is the easier of the two. Why? Seeing the Negotiation Boxes in which *you* live requires strong awareness of others as well as accurate self-awareness. That is why the transition from three to four is such an obvious demarcation between an egocentric, self-focused worldview and a broader one. At four years, you began to accommodate awareness of what others were trying to achieve (e.g., Mom's goals for nutrition and simplicity), which was certainly different from what you hoped to achieve (the goal of autonomy in choosing what you eat).

Take a few minutes now to deconstruct a Negotiation Box you built. Think of someone close to you with whom you interact regularly. Someone you live with or work with works best. I invite you to write that person's name in the diagram below or in the center of a separate sheet of paper. Now, think about a situation in which the two of you do an activity together. At home, that might be watching TV, sleeping in the same bed, doing housework or yard work—so many choices! At work, that might be driving to a job site, preparing for a meeting, picking orders in a warehouse, planning an event, going on a business trip together, or stocking shelves...you name it!

What are the agreements and limits in this activity? Ahhh...but before we deconstruct this Negotiation Box, one more note about limits and agreements. Remember, each category includes three subtypes: cultural/social, interpersonal, and intrapersonal. Culture/society creates agreements about what we all expect from one another. Interpersonal agreements and limits are forged with others based on what you each want and don't want. Intrapersonal agreements and limits are those you establish within yourself.

So, back to the box. In the relationship and situation you're thinking about, what are the limits and agreements already existing, perhaps only at the subconscious level? Opening your mind to the cultural, interpersonal, and intrapersonal sources of limits and agreements, fill in this image of a Negotiation Box to see all the details together:

```
              Agr:_____      Lim: _____
Agr:_____    ┌─────────────────────────┐    Lim:_____
                             │   Person in the Box:    │
Lim:_____    │                         │    Agr:_____
                             │                         │
Agr:_____    │  Situation of the Box:  │    Lim:_____
                             │                         │
Lim:_____    │                         │    Agr:_____
                             │                         │
Agr:_____    │                         │    Lim:_____
                             │                         │
Lim:_____    └─────────────────────────┘    Agr:_____
              Agr:_____      Lim: _____
```

Feel free to add limits and agreements not in place now that you see you'd like to add. Define the box as it exists now and/or how you would like it to be. Do you have some limits that haven't been respected and so you have simply abandoned them?

Here's an example of how such a box might look, for something as simple as choosing a restaurant for dinner with my mom:

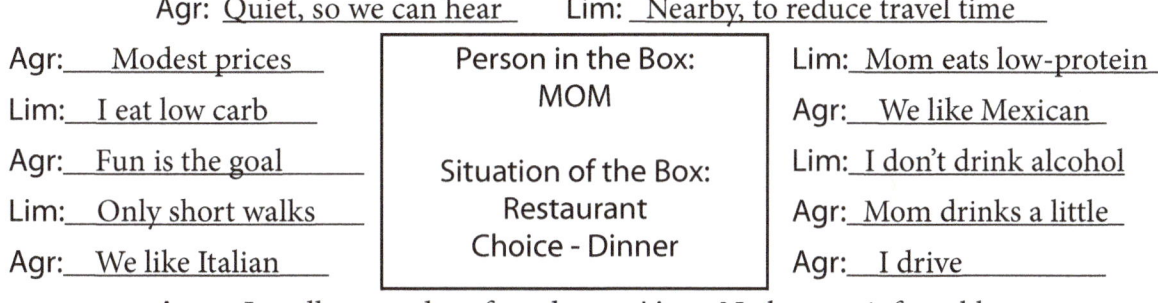

In this case, it doesn't matter which of us is inside this box making the decision about where to eat; all the same limits and agreements apply. You might have noticed that almost all our yes and no items are interpersonal or intrapersonal. "I drive" can be considered a cultural agreement because Mom, by her late eighties, had given up her license and car.

Once you see how these Negotiation Box–building principles work, you will become more conscious of your power to negotiate within the confines of the boxes you're in. You can also be more transparent about building Negotiation Boxes for others.

What Do You Want?

For many of us adults, the real work of mining this Treasure of Negotiation lies in learning to know what we really want. Most of us have been inundated our whole lives with stories of what others think we *should* want, of what will win us the love and approval of others if only we were to want *that*. From our earliest days, we've invested time and energy learning to discern what will prevent rejection by those we love. We are so full of these *stories* of wanting specifically identified things—deemed "appropriate" for our gender, religion, skin color, or station in life—that we really don't know how to answer the most basic question, "What do you want?"

The Treasure of Negotiation cannot be mined and polished fully without the emotional intelligence that comes from mining Trust, Independence, and Faith. Let's say my Treasure mining has gone smoothly and I have learned: 1) I can get my needs met in the world; 2) I am (as is every other person I know) unique unto myself, and that reality is internal unless I share it; and 3) there is a purpose for me—life calls me to do something on behalf of a greater vision. From this foundation, I will trust myself—my instincts and intuition, my desires—and I will be able to recognize when a goal is outside of my interests. I will see that an external story is being foisted upon me, perhaps by someone of good intention but still foisted. I will be able to recognize, "This is not really what I want; this is what *she/he* wants."

If, on the other hand, my mining work has been less than fully supported and less than successful, then I may have learned: 1) my needs don't matter and don't get met; 2) I only know how I feel when I see how others feel or someone else tells me how I *should* feel; and 3) life is a daily grind of meeting responsibilities and that's all there is to it. In this case, I likely will struggle to determine what I want or need unless somebody else affirms that.

So, if you don't already have the answer to, "What do you want?" then it's time to start finding out. The two tools offered below—Dipsticking and the Art of Postponement—are tools for this purpose. Among many assets from my years with an incest survivors' therapy group, the seeds of both these tools were planted in that group's discussion. Of course, I can't give individuals credit for their ideas, or I would violate the confidentiality of the group. At more than thirty years removed from the experience, I'm not even sure I could tell you who first brought us these ideas. Let me say, in general, those women were some of the toughest, as well as some of the most vulnerable and brave, people I've ever met. I learned a great deal from each of them, all of which has proven to be of deep and lasting value.

Dipsticking. If you don't know what you want, listen to your body. It knows. Young children always know how they feel because they literally *feel it*, physically or physiologically, in their bodies. They may not yet have the words to describe or name it for us. "My fists are balled up, my biceps are tight, my jaw is clenched, and my intestines are rolling," might lead an adult to provide the name of the emotion "anger" for that set of *feelings* in the body. Our adult vocabularies still include the word *anger*, but it may be disconnected completely from the physical feelings. If you tell me, "I'm so angry!" but aren't feeling these body signals, then *angry* is a thought, not a name for your actual feelings.

The idea of the dipstick is to send a little measuring tool down into the body. It's a conscious journey to notice where the body is expressing *feelings*, mostly with muscular, hormonal, or sensory disequilibrium. Where is there tightness, rigidity, or sudden lack of strength? What juices or energies are flowing? Is your face hot, or have your hands suddenly turned to ice? What are your body's signals? If somebody wants to kiss me and I feel sick to my stomach…umm…maybe I should say no.

For some folks, dipsticking might be as easy as a shift of focus from the mental to the physical. For those of us who experienced physical or sexual violation of our bodies in childhood, or have other kinds of body dysphoria, that shift of focus is not so easy. The body may have been disregarded, ignored, and its messages intentionally blocked with food, drugs, alcohol, or dissociation for years—or decades. The body may have become something extraneous, unwanted, that must be dragged unwillingly through the rigors of life. Learning to reconnect with this body, to love it, to care for it as it was not cared for in childhood, to listen to its communications—all this comprises a substantial recovery task for those with histories of sexual and/or physical assault. In those cases, therapy with a licensed clinician may be a helpful addition to your Development Do-Over journey.

The Art of Postponement. What if, in the pressure of the moment, or because I'm still working on that recovery work of reconnecting to my body, I can't make the dipstick work quickly enough for a prompt response? What if I need ten minutes alone to relax, breathe, and be intentional about focusing on my body's messages? In that case, postponing a reply is always an option. Develop the Art of Postponement to give yourself time to know what you really want, how you really feel. Whenever you can, delay an answer you feel uncertain about. This postponement tool can be effective in workplaces as well as in family and other personal relationships.

Here's how it works: You don't have to respond immediately in many situations where you might seem to be on the spot. This reality is especially true in employment situations. Depending on your role, relative to who's asking and depending on the situation, you might try one of the following options or their many variations:

- I'll get back to you with my decision in ten minutes/half an hour/tomorrow (as appropriate).
- Let me think about that for a bit and I'll let you know by ___ (name a time).
- Let me check my calendar/check with my team/check what that report from management says…before I give you an answer.
- I need a few minutes; let me call you right back.

Of course, you don't want to overuse this tool and be the jerk who never responds without a break. Don't answer your partner's, "Do you want toast or cereal?" with "Let me think about that for a bit and I'll let you know by 7:15," that is, unless you're *trying* to shorten your relationship using passive-aggressive strategies.

The heavy, pickaxe level of mining your Treasure of Negotiation has two parts, like the axe. The wide chopping blade is the understanding that Agreements and Limits—your yes and your no muscles—are not the same as your boundaries—the edges defining the essence of who you are. Exercising these yes and no muscles consistently will, ultimately, strengthen your boundaries. But limits and boundaries are *not* the same thing.

The more you establish agreements and limits based on how you really feel, on what you really want, rather than from reflex, obligation, or fear, the stronger your boundaries become. The healthier your boundaries (remember the three-quarter moons), the easier it becomes for you to know what you want in a negotiation.

The sharp, pointed end of the pickaxe head is the ability to see the limits and agreements defining the edges of your choices, and then seeing all the options you have inside a Negotiation Box. Once you get Negotiation's raw ore out of your internal bedrock, the refinement work is this: learn to ask for something *you* want, which fits in someone else's Negotiation Box for you.

The ***Childhood Treasure*** of Negotiation opens a whole new world to a sociable little four-year-old, and it will for you too, as an adult creating a Development Do-Over. Remember, the job of a four-year-old is to begin understanding how her edges—her boundaries—fit up against the boundaries of other people in her world. If you never figured that out and have, all your life so far, been run over by others, or been the one running over others, there are other options!

In addition to the tools of Dipsticking and the Art of Postponement, I offer you my number one tool: *Seek always the wisdom of childhood.* Any time you can, keenly observe children who are between about eight or nine months and about four years of age. Watch them from an objective distance as they play and interact with others. Notice how they always know quickly what they want. See the strength of their emotions when they 1) want something yet take no action; 2) want something and ask for it; 3) want something and are thwarted in getting it; or 4) want something and ask/cajole/manipulate/tantrum to get it.

With a little practice, you will be able to see the emotional weathers moving across the surfaces of these little human planets. Watch the facial expressions, listen for the tones of voice, see the body postures, the tensing of muscles, the drawing in or flailing of body parts. Through observation, learn to recognize the physical indicators of various emotional states in children. Why? So you will recognize them in yourself as indicators of when you want something and are or aren't getting it.

Cut the Facets of Your Vision

As we begin the Development Do-Overs to bring Vision into the construction of our Little Red House, we become the makers of our own way in the world. With Vision anchoring one side of the roof, rarely will you feel the need to throw up your hands in resignation and surrender to one of life's typical problems. With Vision in your safe home, you become your first resource to solve your own problems. You become the chief designer of your world. Once we have Vision glittering in our rooftop's eave, we begin to see how we are the drivers of these vehicles that are our lives.

Was your mining for Vision not sufficiently supported by your family? Here's how you might know:

- **Do you procrastinate**, even on simple tasks? Maybe this shows up as putting off the big things like repairs or spring cleaning. Maybe it looks like letting the dishes pile up in the sink or letting dust bunnies grow to the size of minivans under your bed. Procrastination can also look like failure to meet legal obligations like filing tax returns and paying property taxes—not because you don't have the money, but because you just can't seem to sit down and get the paperwork done.
- **Do you obsess over details?** Perhaps you set out to clean up the kitchen by unloading the dishwasher, reloading it, and washing the sinks. Before you know it, you've been digging gunk from under the stove rings with a toothpick for twenty minutes and the dishwasher hasn't been unloaded yet. Or do you sit down to write a note of sympathy to a friend who's lost a loved one, throw thirty false starts in the trash because you can't find the perfect words, and never send the note at all?
- When you're working toward a goal or project conclusion, **do you frequently feel that you're spinning your wheels?** Maybe you get focused on some minutiae of the process and miss a big step. Perhaps you make pretty good progress for a while and then languish on a step you can't get completed. Or maybe you can't figure out what steps lead to your goal or what order to do the steps in.

- **Do you have trouble forming a goal and/or a plan to achieve it?** Do you often start projects but not complete them? Perhaps you struggle to envision the end-state your goal will achieve. Maybe you can see the goal but have no idea how to organize your approach to it. Or maybe, like me, you start a handicraft project as a gift, but the occasion comes and goes while you're still trying to get it done.
- **Are you unable to think "outside the box"?** Do you find yourself looking at a problem to solve or a hurdle to overcome and seeing only one or two possible solutions, neither of which look good to you? Are you often stuck with the most common options or the ones your parents would have used?
- **Do you feel helpless about achieving goals?** ("This is too hard!") Perhaps you see the goal and have a plan, but the barriers and challenges to your progress loom too large and seem insurmountable. Maybe you have a plan with steps so large and complex you can't see how to complete even the first one. Or do you get stymied right from the start, tripped up by a lack of faith in yourself?

If any of these challenges with setting and achieving goals plagues you, then mining the Treasure of Vision is your work. Remember, Vision is the place where Big Ideas are born and are then shepherded into life. If one or more of the patterns above permeate your life, then let's get digging!

Most five-year-olds have no trouble coming up with a Big Idea, in fact, many Big Ideas. Especially if they managed to fully mine and polish the Treasure of Faith, they have positive experiences with tackling what seems impossible. While three-year-olds' Big Dreams are about long-term ways to change the world for the better, fives' Big Ideas are more immediate and practical. They see a problem before them—like a lot of birds living in a little wooded area with no water source in it—and they want a quick solution.

Do you already hatch Big Ideas but through procrastination, disorganization, or lack of motivation simply fail to execute them? If not, if you also find yourself void of exciting Big Ideas, then return to your work from the White Queen exercise (pp. 80-84).

Which of those "White Queen's Impossible Things to Imagine" that you dreamed up has a step that could be immediately executed? Is there a first step you could tackle with a plan, if you knew how to make and follow a plan? You see, Big Ideas and the plans that achieve them occur regularly on that spiral path to a Big Dream.

Perhaps your Big Idea is freedom from cigarettes, drugs, or alcohol. Maybe it's a new job, moderate eating of healthy foods, or a healthier relationship with your sister or partner. Is it a routine of daily exercise or daily practice of journaling? A published novel? Starting a business?

Identify one Big Idea you wish to realize, to welcome into your life, and write it here or in your journal. Be specific and concrete. What will change?

My Big Idea is: _____

_____

Map of Promise

Here's the thing: The idea is not usually the hardest part. The plan and its execution are typically the harder components of Vision for most of us. To support you in mining this Treasure now, I recommend completing the **Map of Promise**. Adapted with permission from colleague Rob Bocchino's Map of Change, this tool helps you visualize all aspects of the path to your Big Idea. The simplest design for a Map of Promise involves a sheet of paper and a pen or pencil. The bigger the paper, the more room you'll have to map out all the parts. I recommend 11" by 17" if you can lay your hands on a sheet.

You're also welcome to work in a larger or smaller medium if that works better for you. Lay out the Map on your basement floor with masking tape or across your backyard with tree branches if you like. Use big paper and crayons or markers, or use smaller paper and fine-tip drawing pens. Do whatever you like to create a concrete visual image of your Map.

The first step is to place two boxes on your Map near the edge(s) of your space; one is for where you are Now, and the other represents the future time When you've achieved your Big Dream. Label these two boxes as the "Now" (present) and "When" (future) of your Map. Maybe your Map will be as simple as this one at this point in the process:

To anchor those two locations in time and place, in preparation for the next steps, try the following meditative process. Stand in a largish space where you have some room to move. Imagine that the When box—the future point when your goal is reached—is a square around your feet on the floor or ground. Stand in your When box and imagine and feel what it's like to live with your Big Idea accomplished. When you stand in When—feet solid on the ground, back straight, and breathing calmly—and pretend you are already there, how do you feel? What are your emotions? Breathe deeply and feel these emotions for a moment. Let your heart fill with them. Standing in this future, imagining your Big Idea well-established, what are your thoughts about yourself and the world? What are the words in your head? Breathe and listen for a moment to the thoughts you will have when you reach this future When. Let words waft lightly through your mind. How does your body look and what do you do, how do you act, as you live with this goal realized? What is your posture? How do you move? How does your body feel? Feet firmly rooted in the When, let the rest of your body move as you notice your muscles and bones. As you imagine all the ways in which this new pattern affects your life, add your projections of how it will affect the lives of those you care about. Think about how the implementation of your Big Idea will positively change your relationships at home and at work. Who will appreciate your change? Who will it be easier to be with? Who will want to spend more time with you? Now integrate all these experiences of the *When*. Experience in all possible ways how great it feels to be in this future with your dream realized. Breathe into it; believe in it.

Now, turn to your physical map and take a few minutes to create this new pattern—in writing, in imagery you draw, or in some other medium. Represent this new pattern in words or images clearly describing what you just experienced as "Job done!" Capture it so you will always remember the fullness of that experience.

Once you are satisfied with your representation of When, return to your meditative creation process. Stand in the When box again, briefly, and reconnect with your experience of how it will be with this new part of your life. Now step out of the When box and walk however far you need to, and in whatever pattern seems right, until you find yourself standing where you think your Now is relative to When. You may find Now seems to be not too far away from your future When…or that it is very far indeed. You may find the path between them is a simple straight line or that it is filled with bends and curves. Once you feel you have reached the right place, stand still. Imagine a little box defining the space around your feet at this exact moment in time as Now.

Stand here and fully experience how it feels to be in *this* place and time in contrast to how it felt to have achieved what you so desire. When you stand within your life today—feet solidly on the ground, spine erect, breathing, and calm—when you acknowledge you are not living in that future with your goal realized, how do you feel? What are your emotions? Breathe deeply and feel these emotions for a moment. Feel your heart full to the brim and overflowing with the emotions of Now. Standing in life as it is today, recognizing it as a well-established reality that does not include your Big Idea, what are your thoughts about yourself and the world? What are the words in your head?

Breathe and listen for a moment to the thoughts you have Now. Let words and phrases float through the windows of your mind. How does your body look, what do you do, and how do you act as you live life before your goal is reached? What is your posture? How does your body feel? Rooted in this Now, also notice how you move; notice your body's rhythms.

As you fully feel your current life, add your knowledge of the impact you now make on the lives of those you care about. Think about the impact of life without your Big Idea. How does its absence affect your relationships at home and at work? Who resists or stays away from you? Who feels comfortable with you as you are? Who wants you to stay in this Now? Who wants you to change? Fully aware of this life without the fulfillment of your Big Idea, describe this life in writing, in imagery you draw, or in some other medium on your Map.

Now that you have experienced When and Now and recorded them on your Map of Promise, use your imagination to, once again, experience that When space. Look at how you captured When on your Map and remember how it felt to stand in When, living your dream. Stay with that feeling, breathing into the fullness of it. Next, mentally step back into Now and feel yourself as you are now but add your yearning for When. The experience is often stronger if you go back to the spot that was your Now space and embody all your feelings again rather than just thinking about it.

Standing in Now, let yourself feel how much you wish you were in your When. Feel your longing for that life as you experienced it in your imagination. Now, reach out for When—literally, reach; from the depth of your desire for When, stretch your arms, your mind, and your heart toward that future. Whether it is close to Now or far away, look at the space separating your Now from your When, and know you can build a way to span that gap. (This knowing comes to you from the Treasure of Faith, by the way.) If you don't yet feel that certainty, imagine for now that you can create a pathway of simple, easy-to-take steps to eventually lead you from Now to When.

Feel your desire for your When, gently pulling you out of your Now. Stretch your arms toward When and imagine taking the first step. As you embody this experience, literally allow your reaching arms, mind, and heart to pull you into a step forward toward When. Lean so far toward When that you must step forward or fall.

There. You started building the span across that unknown gap between where you are now and where you want to be. Look down at your feet at this first step and let yourself know what it is. Take whatever "crazy" thing your mind thinks up first. Now you know your first step.

Next, go back to that space where you stood for When. Stand there and face the future. Feel again how you live in this reality of goal accomplished. Now, turn around and look at the ground right behind you. What was the last step you took, which delivered you to this destination?

From the first step out of Now, you may also be able to see another couple of early steps, and from your last step into When, you may see a step or two that came before that last one. Record all these steps as you see them.

Perhaps now, your record of your map looks more like this one:

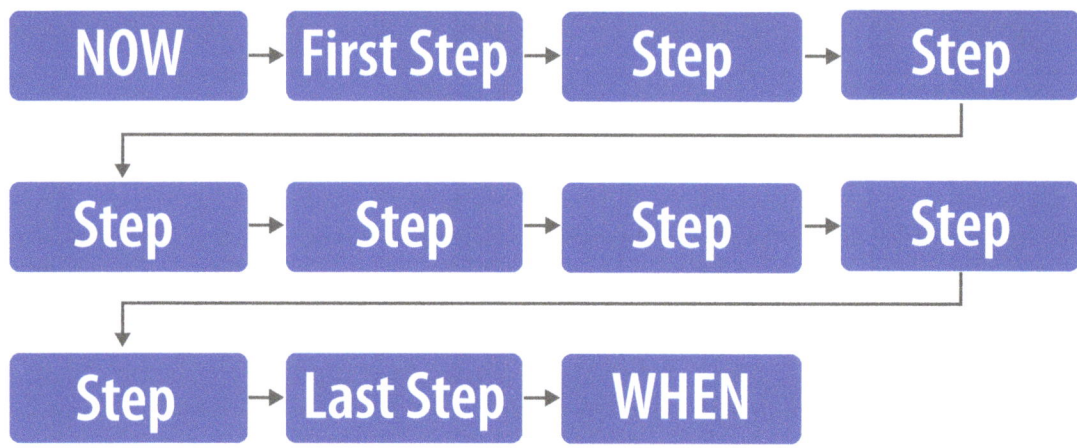

Once you know the first steps forward out of Now and the last few steps that will deliver you to When, it's time to pause and consider the environment in which we are planning. Do you face barriers to your effort? Are there people or conditions that might appear to block your progress or slow you down? Are there doubters, including yourself? Is there an apparent lack of resources to enable your next step? Take a few minutes to meditate on these potential challenges and depict them on your map in whatever way makes sense to your intuitive self. They might manifest as brick walls, big piles of rock to climb, fire, or a fierce Samurai swinging swords at you. Let your mind float, finding the possible barriers to your journey from Now to When. Beware! Some barriers might wear the faces of loved ones.

Are there also supports for what you're trying to achieve? People or conditions that will appear along your way to prosper and propel you? Do you benefit from others' help with your efforts? Do you have champions who cheer you on, including yourself? Do you realize there is an abundance of resources to ensure your success? As images on your map, they might appear as angel-made ropes, lowered from the heavens; sturdy beams that hold up a span of bridgework; or a trampoline that lets you jump over a wall. Again, take a few minutes to reflect on these possible supports and depict them on your map.

Your finished map may look something like this.

Make the Map of Promise yours. The more you let yourself really engage with it, the more meaningful it will be for you. Get out crayons, markers, or colored pencils (borrow or buy some if you don't have any; it's fun to use color!) and allow the child in you to draw with abandon. Release all your worries about artistic skill or appearance. This is a tool, a gift from your deepest self to your human mind. Relax and trust that you are receiving a loving endowment and let the images flow from your heart onto the page.

Once you finish your map, find a way to keep it close to you in your life. Hang it near the bathroom mirror, carry it in your ever-handy journal, take a photo of it with your phone, or if your lifestyle accommodates it, paint it onto the basement floor or lay it out in masking tape. Be creative! The point is to let your map be a daily…well, map: a map you can actually follow, like a GPS map. Just as a smartphone app can alert you to barriers like accidents and rush hour traffic, or help you find support resources along the way—hospitals, gas stations, Starbucks locations—your Map of Promise can be your daily guide to reach your Big Idea.

I can testify to the usefulness of this tool because this book started out as a Big Idea and a Map of Promise. This ability to see a goal—to have a vision of something BIG that you want, something that seems above the limit of your reach—is what your five-year-old self had in abundance. A successful mining of Vision, as a **Childhood Treasure**, creates in us the capacity to see the path to the goal. Perhaps, more importantly, it also builds in us the courage, self-love, and self-confidence to march ourselves along that path, accept graciously any gifts of support, and find a way around, under, over, or through barriers.

You may not be surprised to hear that, the more you mine the first four Treasures, the easier this one is to pry from the matrix rock. Once you have fully mined, faceted, and polished up this gem, your generativity and productivity expand exponentially, as you stop telling yourself, "Oh, I can't do that. I could never do that."

Smooth Out Your Compromise

Do you remember my description of that pulsing respiration of individuation (p. 31) from one to four years—out and moving back in, leaving home-base security for the unknown and then hustling back—remember? Remember that I said the return to home base never really stops? Yet the exhaling expansion from Negotiation into Vision—from four to five years of age—begins an opening outward that continues, pulsing ever farther outward for many years. Actual returns to home base become fewer and fewer, while we rely increasingly on connecting in memory or sentiment.

Then, at the still-tender and vulnerable age of six years, rather than do another rebound to the safety of parental home base, your next step outward was into a world where you were expected to be much more on your own. Shockingly, it is also a world in which real sacrifice is required. You think I'm kidding? Listen, my friend, kindergarten is an entirely new field of endeavor and one in which your tools may no longer be the best or the strongest. Why do you think kids cry on the first day of kindergarten?

Lots of folks say you can't get everything you want in life. This childhood wisdom from your sixth year is even carved into the musical history, thanks to the Rolling Stones. As Mick Jagger's voice sings in my mind, "You can't always get what you wah-ant," my collection of my crystals of Compromise vibrates in resonance. But, as the Stones also told us, "If you try sometimes, you might find, you get what you need."

There, in a succinct little nutshell, is the **Childhood Treasure** of Compromise. You can't always get everything you want, but if you're willing to compromise, you will likely get what is most important to you. The wisdom of the Treasure of Compromise might also be referred to as the "Wisdom of the Pack." Young puppies, with the help of the Alpha female and other members of their pack (including the human ones), learn when they should keep pursuing their puppyish curiosity and when they should roll onto their backs and submit. They will never be starved or physically threatened in a healthy pack, but they will learn when and *how much* to compromise their individual interests to the will of the pack.

Here's a little checklist to help you get a sense of your capacity for Compromise. Again, this is not a valid or reliable psychometric assessment. Don't think too long about any one item, just mark a check or "X" for your gut response and move on.

	Often	Sometimes	Rarely
When you want several things in a situation, do you push to get them all, even if others must compromise or surrender to make that happen?			
When your interests conflict with those of a loved one, do you surrender your interests so they can have what they want?			
When you know you can't have everything you want, do you default to the one thing that's easiest to achieve?			
Do you get into conflicts with friends, family, and coworkers that become unresolvable, causing permanent rifts?			
Do you carry some resentment toward friends and coworkers who seem to always get what they want?			
Are you mostly focused on the differences between yourself and others rather than the ways you are the same?			
Do you find you don't understand what others want, and they don't understand you either?			

	Often	Sometimes	Rarely
Are you uncomfortable in a diverse group of people, where there are few or no other people like you?			
When every member of a small group wants something different, do you find it hard to see the common ground?			

Tally the Xs in each column and enter the totals: _____ _____ _____

The simple scoring is this: If most of your marks are in the Often and Sometimes columns, you need this Development Do-Over!

The Power of Choice

The adult's return to the mining of this *Childhood Treasure* is all about cultivating the power of choice. There is always a choice to be made in a compromise. Each of us must answer, for ourselves, the essential question, "What am I willing to let go of in favor of what higher priority?" We must ask ourselves this question hundreds of thousands of times—each time our needs and desires are not in close alignment with those of others with whom we are in relationships.

At four, Negotiation was a fairly basic approach to getting along with others. At six, Compromise also required you to know your limits and the kinds of agreements you wanted to forge with others. At six, though, you also had discovered the goals your Vision called you to. As you began more and more to live your life in honor of your commitments to your goals, your power of choice also expanded.

It's counterintuitive, I know, but true. Deeper commitment expands choice.

Think of it this way: Without exercising your power of choice, you are left to one of only a few other options: 1) complete anarchy, 2) rigid adherence to rules wherever you can find them, or 3) attempting to please everyone who matters to you. If none of these sounds good to you, then consider choice as a lifestyle. The most challenging aspect of this path is truly believing you always have a choice.

There is one caveat: You don't get to decide when or how to die (unless you take your own life, and I hope you never make that choice). Otherwise, *everything* else in your life involves a choice. You don't believe me? Here are some life activities/events that folks in my workshops have proposed as choiceless, and my understanding of the choice being made:

Proposed Choiceless Activity	Hidden Choice Being Made
Going to work every day	Paycheck and benefits vs. none
Paying your taxes	Being fined and/or jailed vs. not
Paying your mortgage	Keeping your home vs. losing it
Feeding your children	Keeping your children vs. losing them

What other choiceless activities would you propose? Can you see the hidden choice you are really making?

The Treasure of Compromise gives you a world of freedom: enough structure for safety, without rigidly adhering to rules or driving yourself nuts with people-pleasing. Compromise lives in the balance between achieving your desires and allowing for others to achieve theirs as well. The relationship skills that support compromise go beyond the simple binary of yes/no, beyond the basic limits/agreements that were possible with Negotiation at age four. Compromise is much more than the simplicity of a four-square Negotiation Box. It is more of a porous mesh safety net you weave as you simultaneously use it.

Guided Choice

The essential components of Compromise that guide your choices are your values and commitments. Do you know what those are in your life? Let's examine the latter first, as they may be easier to see.

To whom in your life do you have commitments, implied or explicit? If you have a spouse or partner, you may have made a commitment to him/her for monogamy between you. If you have a child, the decisions to give birth and keep the child committed you to rear it: feed, clothe, house, and protect him or her until he or she is an adult…and often far beyond that point. If you have accepted employment, then you have committed to show up and do your job to the best of your ability. Maybe you've made some commitments to yourself. I once knew a man who had committed to himself to write his mother-in-law a letter every week, and he did so faithfully every Sunday of her life, mailing them on Mondays.

What are your commitments in life? Take a moment to make a list and start by identifying the most significant relationships in your life, where commitments are likely to exist. A few possible relationships are listed below to get you started:

Relationship	Commitment
Spouse/partner	
Parent(s)	
Sibling(s)	
Employer	
Child(ren)	
Self	

You may want to reflect on each of these commitments for a moment from the perspective of how you have compromised to maintain it. What have you given up—not with resentment, but with quiet contentment—to enjoy the benefits to you that also come with this obligation? Shine up your Compromise gem by simply noticing the *willing* compromises you make to maintain the commitments you already have. Then, yes, also make note of the ones you resent, if any. Take careful note, too, of the ones that were not explicit. You and your partner didn't actually *discuss* and clearly commit to monogamy? Then it's not a commitment you can count on, in yourself or in your partner.

Now let's look at your values. Two of the simplest measures for your values are your check register/credit card statements and your calendar. How you spend your money and time are good metrics for what you value. Are your biggest monthly expenditures on entertainment? On alcohol and/or recreational drugs? Your tithe to your spiritual community? Decorating your home? Putting your children through college?

Think of the minutes in your days as another kind of coin you spend. Where do you most heavily invest the value of your time? At work? With your children? Doing volunteer work? Watching TV? Scrolling on social media? Cleaning and organizing your stuff?

Take a moment to make a record of the top five categories of expenses in your monthly budget and the top three ways you spend the hours of your days. Notice if there is anything you want to change about those lists. Then, tuck them away to recheck them six months from now. Check them again a year after starting the Development Do-Over strategies below.

These data clearly show you some of your values—where you invest your time and money. These are your Expressed Values. How do you like the picture those measures paint? Are your money and time investments feeling comfortable and "right" to you?

Next, putting aside these Expressed Values, let's discover what your heart and mind say about values. Look at the list of possible values below and pick about half of them (twenty-seven) that you value most:

- ☐ Acceptance: to be accepted as I am
- ☐ Achievement: sense of accomplishment
- ☐ Advancement: moving forward in my career
- ☐ Adventure: frequent risk-taking
- ☐ Aesthetics: studying or appreciating beauty
- ☐ Autonomy: working independently
- ☐ Belonging, involvement, community
- ☐ Caring, love, affection
- ☐ Challenge: full use of your potential
- ☐ Change and variety
- ☐ Compassion: caring for others
- ☐ Competition: pitting my abilities against others
- ☐ Cooperation: working with a team
- ☐ Courage: standing up for my beliefs
- ☐ Creativity: being imaginative, innovative
- ☐ Democracy
- ☐ Ecological awareness, health of the earth
- ☐ Economic security: having enough money
- ☐ Excellence: striving to be the best
- ☐ Excitement
- ☐ Fame, renown, distinction
- ☐ Family happiness, relationships with family

- ☐ Freedom, independence, liberty
- ☐ Friendship: close personal relationships
- ☐ Happiness, fun, enjoying life
- ☐ Health: physical and psychological well-being
- ☐ Helping people in a direct way
- ☐ Helping society, contributing to the world
- ☐ Honesty: telling the truth as I know it
- ☐ Hope: being positive and optimistic
- ☐ Inner harmony: being at peace with myself
- ☐ Integrity: living my values, behaving ethically
- ☐ Intellectual status: being regarded as an expert
- ☐ Justice, fair treatment for all
- ☐ Knowledge gained through study and experience
- ☐ Leadership: initiation of action; being a model
- ☐ Leisure: having time for hobbies, interests
- ☐ Loyalty, commitment, dependability
- ☐ Nature, preserving/enjoying the natural world
- ☐ Nonviolence, world peace
- ☐ Order, structure, organization, systems
- ☐ Pleasure, enjoyment
- ☐ Power, authority, influence
- ☐ Purpose, meaning, direction in life
- ☐ Responsibility, reliability, being accountable for results
- ☐ Recognition: acknowledgment for contributions
- ☐ Safety: physical and personal security
- ☐ Self-respect, self-esteem
- ☐ Solitude: time and space for myself
- ☐ Spirituality, faith, beliefs
- ☐ Stability, predictability
- ☐ Tolerance: accepting or valuing differences
- ☐ Wealth, luxury, having the finer things
- ☐ Wisdom, insight, enlightenment

Now take that list of twenty-seven and cut it in half again, to about fourteen. Acknowledging that the twenty-seven items you picked are all important values, you're not rejecting half of them. Rather, you are selecting the fourteen most crucial to you.

Now, halve the list again. Select only the seven most important values in your life.

The next step is the hardest. Again, acknowledging these seven values are all very important to you, narrow them down again to just four. Choose the four that, without which, you would not be you. These are your most precious Aspirational Values.

Hang in there for another minute because understanding your values is essential to your Development Do-Over on the Treasure of Compromise. The last step is to compare this list of your four most precious and freely chosen values with the list of values expressed by your life. Do the values you discovered through a review of how you spend your time and treasure line up with your chosen values? Do they seem to express different positions? Here's an example of several gaps I discovered in myself, from my early work with this tool:

Expressed Values	Aspirational Values
Intellectual status: being regarded as an expert	Acceptance: to be accepted as I am
Recognition: acknowledgment for contributions	Belonging, involvement, community
Excellence: striving to be the best	Leisure: having time for hobbies, interests
Fame, renown, distinction	Challenge: full use of my potential

If, like mine, your self-selected values are not the same as your expressed values, then the mining work of Compromise begins with a front-end alignment. Your little life C.A.R. will steer into healthier relationships when your time and treasure are invested in support of your chosen (Aspirational) values rather than in the service of the subconscious, default, inherited, or habitual values (Expressed) you've been supporting.

Value-Driven Compromise

The best way to align your life around your values comes in two stages. If you completed the exercises above, you've done step one. Step two is to focus on no more than four of your most crucial seven values. Pick the four values you feel most passionately about and keep them in front of you all the time—in ways that work best for you. Make a list on a sticky note and post it on your mirror, fridge, or dashboard. Make it a screensaver on your computer, or put a note on your phone and set a daily reminder alarm to read it. Heck, tattoo them on your forearm if you want to; just keep them present in your environment. Remind yourself of them every day and several times a day, if possible.

As you find your life increasingly aligned around the values you selected, there are two strategies to bring your gem of Compromise to its brightest shine. First, once you see the trend lines of your time and money investments leaning toward your chosen Aspirational Values, reexamine your list of interpersonal commitments in the light of your chosen values.

How are your values reflected in these commitments in your life, and how are they not? When you have compromised your values, desires, or preferences in these relationships, have you done so willingly? Did you give some ground but also serve one of your most precious values in the process? Looking at how you work with compromise in your most important relationships is a rich tool for self-discovery.

Second, use what you've discovered in situations when you want several or many things and others in that interaction also have diverse interests that don't line up with yours. When you have clarity about what you want, clarity about what others want, and clarity about your values, then choice becomes so much easier. You simply make your choice about how and how much to compromise *based on your highest values*. The way this works for me now is that my highest Aspirational Value has become compassion and kindness to others (and myself!). Well, many times, what I want pales in comparison to this value, so that makes compromise gentle, if not easy.

Compromise is a sophisticated Treasure, one of the most delicate tools for creation of adult relationships. In turn, Compromise creates gifts for those in the relationship and for everyone affected by that relationship. To mine the full value of Compromise, each of us must first locate, dig up, and process the five Treasures before it.

And so it is, also, for the next step. Only with a shiny Treasure of Compromise anchored in the eave of your Little Red House will you be able to locate and mine the seventh and final ***Childhood Treasure***.

Polish Up Your Acceptance

Now, that big expansion from Negotiation into Vision has continued to carry you, at six years of age, into Compromise. And then at seven, with a mind just barely logical, you exhaled a big developmental sigh and pushed forward one more giant step of expansion. There you were, seven years old and probably going into first or second grade, mining the raw ore of your Treasure of Acceptance.

In cultures all over the world, these first seven years are considered the child's foundation for life, and so they must end with learning to let go. The safe home base must be released to ensure we will be forever connected to it, yet not stay standing in it. We release our grip on the security of certainty, to drive our little C.A.R.s out into the great unknown—relationships. Will our needs still be met? Will our dreams be respected?

Remember, the **Childhood Treasure** of Compromise is, essentially, the understanding that you can't always get everything you want, but if you're willing to compromise, you—and everyone else—will at least be likely to get whatever is most important, of most value. Compromise is the Treasure that helps us make a world that works for everyone.

Then, the Treasure of Acceptance requires you to learn the darker truth that you absolutely will *not* always get even those most important, valuable longings fulfilled. The burden we all share in life is that we must learn to live without what we want, hope for, long for. However, we must continue to live, and even thrive, despite this reality. As one of my work supervisors once said, "Wanting and not getting is good for you. It builds character."

Yes, it would be lovely to return to the womb, where you were in perfect comfort all the time with no effort on your part, where, ideally, you were fed, floated, and kept at the perfect temperature 24/7. This was a period of no demands on your time or energy, and few hassles. Well, you can make that choice if you have enough money to pay round-the-clock caregivers to tend to your flotation tank, IV nutrition, and fluids.

For most of us, that is not possible. Indeed, if given a bit more thought, it's not even desirable. Still, at times in our adult lives, many of us may come to moments where we'd love to have this return to comfort. Overwhelmed, stressed, beyond my ability to cope…for even a moment, I occasionally want to give up, lie down, and have someone pet my fevered brow, murmuring softly, "There, there. It's okay. Rest a minute or two."

Here's the brutal truth: Things will go wrong when seen in the light of your plans for them. You will be *certain* you need a specific job, partner, income, home, promotion…and never achieve it. You will be *convinced* you can't live without someone or something in your life, and then you will need to learn to live anyway, without him or her, without it.

There will be loss—unimaginable loss. And pain. Illness. Injury. There might even be suffering. You may follow all the rules, you may be a very, *very* good person—honest, kind, loving, and generous—and something painful or soul-shattering still can happen in your life.

Note, as an example, who I am as the author making these statements. I was sexually assaulted for fourteen years of my childhood, starting when I was an infant. I'm certain I was a good person at six months of age, and at two years, four years… Being a "good girl" didn't stop the assaults. I still lived and grew and, eventually, thrived as I was intended to.

For some of us, the spiritual or religious aspects of our Treasure of Faith provide a framework and pathway to acceptance as a form of devotion. Surrender to Divine wisdom becomes the highest form of Acceptance. In my spiritual philosophy, the Creator of All can *only* create forward momentum toward the greatest and most perfect expression of itself. The Divine has no barriers for me, no limits. At its heart, this divine life force is impelled toward the "greatest good" for me and for all—but on a timeline beyond my tiny ego's ability to comprehend. Therefore, I must surrender to that wiser timeline, accept that I cannot know the greatest good for all.

In my spiritual philosophy, I believe that the roots of my good and its uppermost leaves are as invisible to me as they would be to a little beetle midway up an old-growth tree's trunk. God's Great Good is the life of the whole forest. My life is from the perspective of that little insect, contained in a few square feet of tree trunk in that endlessly expanding and eternal forest. Therefore, some circumstances that appear in my life—like a heavy rainfall that challenges that insect's grip—may seem bad or wrong to me. But, truly, what can I possibly know about the greater good of the wide forest from my teensy beetle view?

I have moved around my little square of tree bark for enough decades to know that any "bad" event in my life can turn out—sometimes after a year or two; sometimes after a few decades—to be the precursor for tremendously good outcomes I never could have expected. Acceptance allows me to know that appearances are not always what they seem. Acceptance lets me release any passing circumstances—dismiss them, really, as irrelevant—and move on. Rather than make rising and falling circumstances the focal point of my life, I watch them rolling by like a film from the real focal point of my life—my awareness that I am the beetle in the endless forest.

This belief system is a significant factor in my creation of a thriving life in the wake of severe trauma and decades of post-traumatic stress. I understand my early experiences drove me forward in my evolution as a person. I am who I am because of the trauma and recovery. It's that simple. I accept it as a *circumstance* in my life…and move on. Accepting my father's sexual assaults and my recovery work as generative forces in my life has been the end of my own journey to reclaim these **7 Childhood Treasures**.

Please don't hear this as an acceptance of the sexual assault of children. Violating children's bodies in any way is *always* wrong, damaging, and criminal. Always. Period.

And yet, I cannot deny that I am who I am because of my *whole* life, which included that pain. The **Childhood Treasures** would not exist, this book would not have been written, without my healing journey. Without the trauma, there would have been a different journey. But—to be *crystal* clear—I would much rather have become this person, with these gifts and this mission, without those assaults and that pain. Too bad. That's what *was*. Now the history is simply a set of circumstances that have no control over my life. They just happen to be the ones that got me to where I am today.

So, how do you know how well you have mined your Treasure of Acceptance? Which one of these two profiles sounds more like you?

Jumpin' Jinny	Jiminy Cricket
☐ Fret and stew over past errors, running internal videotapes of mistakes and beating yourself up for your behavior. ☐ Still tell the story of how someone hurt you deeply years or decades ago…and it still hurts deeply. You'll never get over it. ☐ Refuse to consider revising the way things are done. Staunchly resist all change. ☐ Resist or rail against change and other non-negotiables in life, such as the autonomy of others' choice ("how *could* s/he?"), the weather, and aging. ☐ Feel unable to influence life; feel passively affected or victimized by it. ☐ Often heard to say, "I had no choice." ☐ Blame problems on a vague or unnamed "they" or "everybody."	☐ Engage with life as a delightful obstacle course, full of diverse opportunities to grow, hone skills, and have fun. ☐ Expect some events on this course will be challenging, even difficult and painful to surmount, and see these impediments as a valuable and useful aspect of the game. ☐ Move through the "bad" on the obstacle course with the same open-hearted curiosity, vulnerability, and willingness as through the "good." ☐ Feel free to fully express all of who you are, knowing that some people will find you appealing, while others will not. Happy to find your tribe and not trying to please everyone. ☐ Feel the power to influence and shape life.

If you're more like Jumpin' Jinny than like Jiminy Cricket, then this is an important Development Do-Over for you. Let's get out our pickaxes and go after Acceptance.

Surrender Betrayal

The essence of mining the Treasure of Acceptance is giving up your stories of betrayal. What Eleanor Roosevelt said of others not being able to "make you feel inferior without your consent" is also true of betrayal. We are each a full participant in *every one* of our stories of betrayal. I know. I hate that too.

Remember the Trust-o-Meter (see p. 55)? That basic measure of Trust you assembled in your first year of life was set to its primary mode of operation between about eighteen months of age and three years. Experiences later in life may have modified or enhanced the basic pattern, but this machine was built by an infant and set by a toddler. If your Trust-o-Meter's operating system hasn't been upgraded since then, your life is probably full of betrayals, large and small.

Betrayal is, in fact, an artifact of the toddler years from the developmental phenomenon known as egocentrism. A toddler's way of looking at the world is not egotistical but egocentric—me at the center of everything. An adult who is egotistical operates as if she wants to be the center of everyone's *attention*. A toddler operates with the certain knowledge that he is the center of everyone's *intention*.

Despite the label of Terrible Twos applied to this age group, this way of looking at the world is not bad or evil—or even very terrible. It's a normal stage of development, temporarily created by the development of the physical brain and the evolving organization of the central nervous system.

Toddlers simply cannot see any other perspective but their own. Here's a toddler's essence in five statements:

- Whatever I am thinking, I know you're thinking it too.
- Whatever I want, I know that you want it *for me* as much as I want it for myself.
- Whatever emotion I am feeling, I know you are feeling it too.
- Wherever I hurt in my body, you hurt in yours too.
- You know exactly what's going on inside of me at every moment, as clearly as I know it myself.

So, imagine how easy it is to betray toddlers! Think of how disloyal others must seem when they reveal a different agenda, a different way of thinking or feeling, or desires contrary to the toddler's. Imagine how deceived toddlers feel when they are told "No!" What? Don't you want for them exactly what they want for themselves? Why in the world would you refuse them anything?

We're *supposed* to pass through egocentrism into the next stage, where we lose that point of view. So, what about now? When someone has different thoughts or feelings than you do about the same event or issue, do you see it as a betrayal? If remnants of this egocentric point of view are still hanging around from your toddler years, they're taking up the space that should be occupied by your Treasure of Acceptance. It's time for a do-over on betrayal.

Toddler Vision. For a moment, pretend you can put on a pair of trick glasses and see the world as you did when you were two years old. Slide those frames on and see through the lenses of egocentrism. Can you see how others are your satellites, little planets, revolving around you, a little sun? See how you are the center of everything?

Notice what you're thinking and know that all those around you are thinking the same thing:

- You believe cilantro tastes like soap and so does everyone else.
- You're a liberal so all the people you like and enjoy being with must also be liberals.
- You think divorce is a sin and are sure of universal agreement with that.

Notice what you're feeling and know that all those around you are feeling that emotion along with you:

- What outrages you obviously also outrages your friends.
- What strikes you mute with wonder should strike your partner in the same way.
- As you grieve over the deaths of the latest mass shooting, you know everyone in the country grieves with you.

Notice what you desire, what you want or need in this moment, and know that everyone you see wants you to have it and wants it for you with the same intensity as your own longing:

- Let your passion for travel fill you with its electricity and know that your new sweetheart is as filled with passion for travel as you are.
- Your longing to see Carhenge in Nebraska surely is shared by your whole family.
- Your biggest goal is to own a large, opulent home overlooking the ocean, so of course, your spouse wants that too.

Adult Vision. Now slide those glasses off and look at the world through your adult eyes. No special glasses needed: your default adult vision is a 20/20 understanding of interpersonal boundaries. Now you can see you are *not* actually the sun at the center. You realize you are just one star, dancing in a universe of stars. See how you and the others around you weave in and out of a pattern that is not of your making? Galaxies and galaxies of stars dancing…

Now, notice what you're thinking, feeling, and wanting, and know all those around you have thoughts, feelings, and longings of their own.

- You have the opinion that some specific president brought our country back from the brink of ruin, and someone else—someone you love deeply—has the opinion that the same president was a crook and a charlatan.
- You feel sad today, while your best friend is jubilant.
- You want the last orange and so does your brother.

As you read the three statements above, your logical mind says, "Well, of course. I know that's all possible—even likely." But do you *live* that? Do you *behave* as if you know that, or are you serially betrayed by friends and loved ones, simply because one of these realities occurs. These circumstances are the exact ones needed to create stories of betrayal that last for months, years, or decades.

So, what are your betrayals? Who among your lifetime of relationships with friends, family, other dear ones, coworkers, and strangers has betrayed you and how? Let's get one or two of those stories out where we can see the details in the light of day, shall we? You can use the framework that follows over and over, for as many ancient betrayals as you're still hauling around in your baggage.

I'll go first, then you. The process begins with who, how, and what.

Who betrayed you? _____

For me, it was Mary (fictitious name), a friend of about a year's duration.

How did she betray you? _____
_____
_____
_____

After I helped care for her children so that she could pursue the training for her new career, she threw me out of her life to secure her marriage to a new boyfriend she met in her first job of that new career.

What, exactly, did this person do? (Name the specifics of the behavior, stripped of all emotion and interpretation): _____
_____
_____
_____

Getting down to "just the facts" of Real Reality (see pp. 72-73), I see that Mary and I, two young, single professional women in our mid-twenties, entered into a verbal agreement to rent-to-buy a home, intending to own it jointly. I believed we were supporting each other in our early careers. For example, I parented her two girls while she was out-of-town in a training program for a new career. Then, in her first job after that training program, Mary found a boyfriend and decided to buy "our" house with him. As real estate agents, they used their knowledge of rental, purchase, and contract law, which I did not share, and evicted me. I lost my half of an investment in a new chimney, for which Mary and I had split the cost, an amount that was significant to me at that stage in my earning potential.

Did Mary betray me? Looking at this bare-bones story with the perspective of decades, I would say no. I held unspoken and, frankly, unrealistic expectations and beliefs about the mutuality of the support. As we had put none of our agreement in writing, we cannot know whether we shared the same understanding of the agreement we had made. Probably we did not. I did not have *any* boundaries in those years, so I am certain I was operating mostly on assumptions about 1) what Mary wanted out of our mutual support, and 2) what Mary understood about what I wanted.

Once you begin to see beyond betrayals, using your adult vision to replace a toddler egocentrism, they often remove the costumes they've been wearing in your old story and reveal themselves as misunderstandings or miscommunications. After years of pulling our betrayal stories around in an increasingly heavy set of luggage, we may find it a challenge to finally admit that many of them were times when we didn't communicate clearly from inside healthy boundaries. Ouch.

So, how to let go of them? Maybe, like me, you pursue acceptance—surrender—as a spiritual practice. If you are so inclined, that approach will greatly help you. If not, the secular perspective is that Acceptance does rewire your neural network. Remember, we create our stories about reality by assigning meaning to incoming sensory data. Another person receiving the same data assigns different meaning and creates a different story. On another day, with a different breakfast under your belt or some happy news from a family member, you might assign different meaning to the exact same sensory data.

Once meaning is assigned, the neural network connections forming that story are strengthened—wired ever more strongly together—with each repetition of your old betrayal story. Every time you tell of your ill treatment at the hands of your sister/father/former boss/brother-in-law/youngest son, your story gets more embedded in your brain. Every repetition deepens the neuron-to-neuron connections of your story.

To make new neural pathways, retell your story of the past *in a new way*. Reinterpret the old data in the light of perspective and greater understanding. Some folks can rewrite their stories using mental effort only. You catch yourself in the old betrayal story, feeling it dragging your energy down, and you stop. You mentally change tracks—literally seeing your train of thought jumping from one track to another in your mind and telling yourself, or your listener(s), your "new understanding" story instead. That's what I did with my "new" story of Mary's behavior in my betrayal example.

An Altar to Betrayal

Some of us find it more effective to make concrete this abstract shift from old story to new. To bring this mental change into the physical world, first create an Altar to the Betrayal. Set up a space, on a shelf or tabletop perhaps, to memorialize the betrayal story. Display items representing the betrayal to you, either actually or metaphorically, and spend a few minutes each day for several days gazing upon them and recalling your story of the betrayal.

Then, over the course of seven or so days, intentionally remove the objects, one or two at a time, replacing them with representations of your new story. Release (give away, throw away) or destroy (tear up, shred, burn) the objects associated with the old story, if you can. Remove each symbol with the specific intention of letting go of the old belief in this event as a betrayal. Leave your new story's altar in place for several days, spending a few minutes with it each day by telling yourself your new story.

Values Revisited

Good news! The rest of your mining for Acceptance was partly accomplished with the work you did to mine Compromise. Knowing your Aspirational Values allows you the freedom—and, some would say, the responsibility—to live your life in alignment with those values rather than in alignment with the resistance and inflexibility of hanging on to old unexamined stories.

Below is a chart comparing life without Acceptance to a life with values-based Acceptance. On the left side are some experiences of a life without this *Childhood Treasure*. On the right side are a few examples of mining and polishing Acceptance using those values you identified. In this case, I've used the values I identified as my highest priorities.

Life Without the Treasure of Acceptance	Values-Based Acceptance
Fret and stew over past errors, running internal videotapes of mistakes and beating myself up for my behavior.	I value compassion, so I forgive myself for past errors because I am human. I am gentle with myself and others. I choose kindness first.
Still tell the story of how someone hurt me deeply years or decades ago, and it still hurts deeply.	I value personal growth and always strive for a more generative life that creates joy. I choose to tell a different story now, one of forgiveness.
Refuse to consider revising the way things are done. Staunchly resist all change.	I value growth, so I will open myself to some small changes, even though uncomfortable.
Resist or rail against change and other non-negotiables in life, such as the autonomy of others' choice, the weather, and aging.	
Feel unable to influence life; feel passively affected or victimized by it.	
Often heard to say, "I had no choice."	
Blame problems on a vague or unnamed "they" or "everybody."	

For practice, I invite you to use the values you identified as highest priority in your life to write statements for the blank cells above. You also may want to write your own responses to replace mine in the top three rows.

This somewhat contrived exercise is the first step. As you continue mining Acceptance, you will find yourself more often, in the moment, turning to your Aspirational Values to guide your behavior. With practice, you will release the need to hold tight to painful, self-destructive thoughts. Remember, you're rewiring your neural network, so repetition of the new stories is important. Each time neurons fire together, their connection grows stronger as they create new pathways to replace the old.

Life With Your 7 Childhood Treasures

There you are. You've begun your work to mine, cut the facets into, and polish all *7 Childhood Treasures*. As you've read, I hope you've done the exercises offered to begin this Development Do-Over journey to gather all your Treasures. Whenever you begin, you will change your life for good. You will build a Little Red House as a home for your Self-governed, Ego-aware, Leading, Free S.E.L.F. and fuel your Choice-Agency-Responsibility mobile.

I'd like to close with a vision of what that S.E.L.F.'s daily life looks like as you drive that C.A.R. out into a world of healthy relationships.

A Day in the Life of a S.E.L.F.

What do relationship interactions look like when at least one of the actors is a Self-governed, Ego-aware, Leading, Free S.E.L.F.? Here are a few snapshots, retaken:

Starting the Day. Partner A, seemingly out-of-the-blue and in a bit of a strangled voice, hollers from the bathroom, "Did you return-ship that shirt yesterday like I asked you to?" Partner B calmly replies from the bedroom next door, "Sure did! Do you need the tracking slip?" Partner A replies in a more normal voice, "Oh, great. I appreciate your help, and yes, thanks, I'll take responsibility for tracking it from here." Partner B's Treasure of Independence allows his or her intellectual boundary to assume that a question is just a question, not an accusation. An emotional boundary holds the words in Partner A's question separate from the vocal tone cues that are harder to interpret. Later, Partner B learns that the out-of-the-blue appearance of the question and the strangled voice resulted from the intersection of a mouthful of toothpaste and an important question that had come to mind after being forgotten several times already.

Settling in at Work. Employee, flying a bit breathlessly into a chair at exactly the start time of the sales meeting, sees Manager frowning. Smiling warmly, Employee says, "Thank you again for the permission to arrive a bit late today to accommodate my partner's early flight." Manager smiles back, "Oh! I thought that was next week... (checking calendar); thanks for the reminder." Employee's Treasures of Trust and Negotiation enable a confident reaffirmation, rather than a fearful defense, of the previously created win-win solution to remind the forgetful Manager. Employee's Treasure of Independence provides the boundaries that hold the social cue of the Manager's frown separate from historical facts.

Morning Break. Coworker A slides into a group around a table and whispers, "Did you hear about J____ in Marketing stealing office supplies?" Coworker B replies gently and kindly, "I can't imagine that could be true. J____ has always been honest and upright. Spreading rumors like that could really hurt J____, both personally and professionally, and it's not really our business. Now, did any of you see that new movie we were talking about last week?" Coworker B has the Treasure of Independence, so the intellectual boundary keeps Coworker A's story separated from significant past experience showing J____ to be honest and upright. The Treasures of Compromise and Acceptance align Coworker B's response to this situation with her/his values for kindness and mutual respect.

Morning Team Meeting. Team Leader opens the agenda with a need to course-correct on a goal that is not on target to be achieved. Team Leader asks for suggested new strategies to reach the goal, and Team Member offers a three-step plan that seems to address the barriers in the current plan. In the conversation that follows, the team significantly modifies the middle of the three steps, and a group consensus builds around the revised version of the plan. Team Leader affirms the revised plan and asks Team Member, "Do you have any comments on the modifications to your suggested plan?" Team Member responds, "No, nothing to add; this looks like a great plan." Team Member's Treasure of Compromise allows for letting go of some of what she or he wants to accommodate some of what other team members want. Boundaries from the Treasure of Independence protect the Team Member's sense of self-worth, so there is no need to be defensive about others' different ideas, nor is there a need to "plant the flag" on her or his original idea as the only viable solution.

Lunch. Two friends meet for a planning session for their upcoming cruise to Alaska. Each brings a vision of ideas, the special sites, or events of interest of highest priorities, and lots of willingness to Negotiate and Compromise. An hour later, they have a plan and can lock in the early bird rates for three tours of shared interest. They are also able to comfortably decide to each participate in some events on their own while the other does something else.

Afternoon Appointment. Colleague A and Colleague B meet to design a new workflow. Colleague A is testy and defensive, signaling his ideas are the best and need no discussion. Colleague B—Treasure of Independence shining brightly—listens, calmly questions, assures without being manipulated or manipulative, and ensures a successful outcome for them both. In this example, many Treasures come together to ensure the performance of the "Leading in my life" function of a S.E.L.F.

Evening Workout. After work, at the gym, Body Builder approaches the only ab crunch machine at the same time as Wellness Seeker. Builder asks Seeker if he'd be willing to let him go first because he needs to pick up his children from child care by 6:30 or pay for overtime. Seeker, remembering a time when Builder stepped aside in a similar time crunch for Seeker, agrees readily in the spirit of Compromise. Sometimes the "give up to get" strategy of Compromise evolves over a span of days, weeks, or even months.

Family Dinner. Adult Child comes over for dinner with Parent, who has worked hard for hours to prepare a delicious meal of favorite childhood dishes the Child no longer eats, having chosen a vegan diet. Child compliments Parent on the beautiful meal, honoring the time and effort so obviously spent on her/his behalf. Child then fills a plate with small portions of the inedible dishes and large portions of those that are vegan…and then only eats the latter, without comment. For this Adult Child, Independence, Compromise, and Acceptance combine to generate this "Leading in my life" response.

And what if the Parent notices and comments or asks about the small portions of some one-time favorites from childhood or on the selective consumption of only some dishes? Then Child takes responsibility and apologizes, "I should have reminded you that I decided to eat a vegan diet when you invited me to dinner. It's a big change, and you're not familiar with the way I eat now. I'm so sorry that I can't enjoy ALL these lovely dishes you made for me, but I did have a great meal, and I feel so loved by your nurturing intention!" Trust, Independence, and Faith in action!

TV Time. Friends have a plan to watch a movie together at Host's home. Host trusts that Visitor won't bail at the last minute—based on a long history of experience—but also has learned not to trust this friend's timeliness. So, Host prepares only snacks that are served at room temp—nothing cold getting warm and nothing hot getting cold while waiting for the always-tardy friend—and keeps busy with another project while waiting for Visitor to arrive. A refined Treasure of Trust keeps Host's expectations realistic. The emotional boundary of Independence separates the fact of lateness from any possibly painful stories about Visitor being disrespectful or uncaring.

Going to Bed. As they both settle in for the night, going through their bedtime routines, Partner A operates from healthy Trust and asks Partner B, "Can you add an errand for me into your day tomorrow?" Partner B, with healthy Treasures of Trust and Independence, replies, "Of course, what can I do for you, my love?" Because Partner A can trust Partner B to be supportive and also set appropriate limits, they can ask for what they want without manipulation, wiles, or strategy of any kind. Partner B, with healthy Treasures of Trust, Independence, Negotiation, and Compromise, knows they can trust Partner A not to make burdensome or frivolous requests at the last minute and knows they can say no or ask for an alteration in plans to make saying yes work better. The respective genders of these two partners matters not at all.

Just Be Your S.E.L.F.

It's time to turn out the lights on a day full of the **Childhood Treasures**. Tomorrow, or soon (if you keep up the mining ops!), you will wake up in your new Little Red House. Fully anchored at every junction with the glittering, brilliant gemstones of the *7 Childhood Treasures*, your house will shelter you from most of life's storms. Don't get me wrong, the storms still will rumble and blow. But you will be able to continue being your Self-governed, Ego-aware, Leading, Free S.E.L.F., living safely in your Treasure-filled home. When any storm abates, you will be able to step out into the sunshine and drive your C.A.R. into healthy relationships, bringing your awareness of the power of Choice, Agency, and Responsibility.

More than any other message in this book, I want you to get this one: You can do this! The work of mining your *7 Childhood Treasures* may not be completed as you read these final words. There may be more digging, cutting, and polishing in your future, especially if your childhood was a traumatic one. And you can succeed! I am one example that *anyone* can become a Self-governed, Ego-aware, Leading, Free S.E.L.F. You've begun, with courage, and soon your life will be transformed.

Keep up the mining work, my friend! I'll see you soon, when we're both out there, gently driving our Choice-Agency-Responsibility mobiles into each other's lives.

Assessment of Boundaries Checklist scores
    Scores under 300—nonexistent to very thin (tissue paper to balsa)
    Scores of 301 to 500—medium thick (cedar shingle to ¼" plywood)
    Scores of 501 to 625—strong, protective (3/4" plywood to steel)

About the Author

Dr. L. Carol Scott is an expert in human development, especially how the first seven years define who we become as adults. She dedicates this expertise to the evolution of your potential, through Development Do-Overs. A nationally known consultant, author, and TEDx speaker, she brings you the wisdom of your earliest years, gathered over decades of her experience in early care and education. Dr. Scott confidently declares that "it's never too late" to re-create a healthy early development.

Along with her professional education and experience with thousands of children, parents, and teachers, you'll benefit from Dr. Scott's personal experience. As she achieved an MA in Early Childhood Education, PhD in Developmental and Child Psychology, and a prominent career, Dr. Scott also pursued her own psychological wholeness. From the varied perspectives of teacher, teacher-educator, leader, policy influencer, speaker, and consultant, Dr. Scott's career is certainly rich in knowledge and experience. Into that professional mastery she has woven a hard-won emotional intelligence, a wide and embracing empathy, and a deep understanding of what creates and sustains healthy relationships for adults. Using her *7 Childhood Treasures* approach, her own Development Do-Overs supported her recovery from multiple Adverse Childhood Experiences (ACEs) in her early years. As one proof point for the power of the work she offers, she shares the story of her recovery from trauma, using the wisdom of early childhood development.

Dr. Scott provides keynote addresses, inspirational talks for faith communities, workshops, seminars, online and college courses, and leadership for the future of human development…your development.

www.ingramcontent.com/pod-product-compliance
Lightning Source LLC
Chambersburg PA
CBHW040043100526
44584CB00033BA/4235